SOVIET TEXTILE DESIGN OF THE REVOLUTIONARY PERIOD

I. YASINSKAYA

Introduction
by John E. Bowlt
with 123 illustrations,
98 in colour

THAMES & HUDSON

First published in Great Britain in 1983
by Thames and Hudson Ltd, London

Typesetting by Spingraf
Printed in Italy by G. Spinelli & C.

Illustration from *Heba*, 1922

Introduction

In April 1923 the artist Varvara Stepanova declared:
Fashion, which used to be the psychological reflection of everyday life, of customs and aesthetic taste, is now being replaced by a form of dress designed for use in various kinds of labor, for a particular activity in society. This form of dress can be shown *only during the process of work*. Outside of practical life it does not represent a self-sufficient value or a particular kind of "work of art."[1]

Stepanova was one of several Russian artists who became especially interested in textile and fashion design in the early 1920s, regarding it as a valuable discipline for the practical application of Constructivist ideas. Textile design, especially as formulated by Liubov Popova and Stepanova and, on a different level, by Sergei Burylin and Oskar Griun, became, along with stage design and porcelain and furniture design, one of the most exciting subjects for artistic experimentation in Moscow, Petrograd, and Ivanovo. Of course, this orientation was encouraged by the Constructivist sentiment that "Art . . . was artificially reheated by the hypocrisy of bourgeois culture and, finally, crashed against the mechanical world of our age. Death to art!"[2] Such ideas accelerated the move away from "pure" art to industrial design, a development that was associated particularly with the activities of the Institute of Artistic Culture in Moscow from 1921 on. It was there, in the fall of 1921, that artists such as Popova and Stepanova and their theoretical supporters, Boris Arvatov, Osip Brik, and Nikolai Tarabukin, resolved that industrial design was a creative medium well suited to the new proletarian society.

However, as with most theoretical pronouncements, the deed rather than the word was the beginning of Constructivism. It is important to remember that the notion of designing textiles and clothes for the new Soviet man and woman derived in part from the general demand to transform the outer appearance of Soviet Russia: it was argued that a new economic, social, and political structure must manifest itself in the actual environment, and Lenin's ambitious Plan of Monumental Propaganda, decreed in April 1918, may be regarded as an important stimulus to the Constructivist aspiration to redesign the whole of reality. Lenin demanded, for example, that "Monuments erected in honor of the tsars. . . be dismantled" and that artists produce "projects for monuments intended to commemorate the great days of the Russian Socialist Revolution."[3] The concrete results of Lenin's plan were far from satisfactory. The bureaucracy of Anatolii Lunacharsky's Commissariat for Enlightenment, which was responsible for implementation of the plan, worked clumsily, and many artists, not the least Vladimir Tatlin, viewed the scheme with grave misgivings. In any case, Lenin perceived "monumental propaganda" in terms of nineteenth-century statuary and neither he nor the public at large was pleased with the Cubo-Futurist structures that suddenly appeared on the streets and squares of Moscow and Petrograd.

Lenin's plan left much to be desired, but it did nurture, or coincide with, many other endeavors to superimpose symbols of the new regime on those of the old. Much has been written about the agit-decorations for buildings and transport produced in connection with the celebrations of May Day 1918 and of the first anniversaries of the Bolshevik Revolution in Moscow, Petrograd, and other cities.[4] Many artists, both avant-garde and moderate, helped to disguise the vestiges of tsardom with brightly colored, often geometric, designs carrying revolutionary images and captions. But this grand pageant seemed strangely out of place to a bewildered and indigent populace whose primary need was for food and clothing, not for avant-garde design. As the old lady in Alexander Blok's poem "The Twelve" (1918) puts it: "What's that poster for, that great big piece of material? It would make quite a few socks for our guys, and none of them has any clothes or shoes."[5]

It is tempting to interpret the positive response of leftist artists to agit-design in the first Revolutionary years as an indication of their staunch support of the new political ideals, but such a deduction is not entirely valid. Most of the Russian avant-garde, at least until 1917, were politically unaware and in any case enjoyed considerable artistic and civil freedom. True, they were regarded as buffoons or worse by the mercantile bourgeoisie, but they traveled freely in Russia and Europe, published numerous uncensored manifestoes, and organized shocking exhibitions and debates. What, then, did they expect to gain from the October Revolution? For some of the more practical artists such as Alexander Rodchenko and Vladimir Tatlin, the Revolution provided an opportunity to take art from private into public spaces — "to reconstruct not only objects, but also the whole domestic way of life";[6] for dreamers such as Kazimir Malevich the Revolution held a messianic, apocalyptic force that Russian philosophers and poets had long discussed; for a few, such as Pavel Filonov, the Revolution did, indeed, present a way to create a more democratic society; but for many, not least Vasilii Kandinsky, the Revolution was an inconvenience that interfered with the efficacy of their artistic lives. In other words, there was no single response, positive or negative, to the Revolutionary events so far as the avant-garde were concerned.

Furthermore, the world of design was not new to the Russian avant-garde. The fixtures for the famous Café Pittoresque in Moscow, often described as the first Soviet bohemian rendezvous, were designed by Rodchenko, Tatlin, Georgii Yakulov, and others in July and August of 1917, that is, without regard to the spirit of agit-art. In the field of textile and clothing design, Alexandra Exter, Malevich, Popova, Olga Rozanova, and others had all designed dresses, purses, cushions, and so forth *before* the Revolution, often with Suprematist motifs, and many of these were shown at the two Contemporary Decorative Art exhibitions in Moscow in 1916-1917. In fact, Natalia Goncharova designed "contemporary ladies' dresses" as early as 1913 for the St. Petersburg couturier Natalia Lamanova, who, in the 1920s, became a leading proponent of the new Soviet dress.

Of course, these were only tentative precedents to the brilliant Constructivist patterns produced by Popova and Stepanova, Exter and Lamanova, Rodchenko and Tatlin, in the early 1920s, and there is no question that the commitment of these artists to a new type of clothing was total. They argued that clothing must present the Soviet man and woman as part of an international community (hence the "anonymous," abstract motifs devoid of local, ethnic images), that it must connect them with industrial civilization (hence the geometric or mechanical motifs), and that it must symbolize emancipation and mobility (hence the frequent application of kinetic forms). Popova's and Stepanova's famous geometric textiles and their industrial or professional clothing (easily identifiable uniforms for sportsmen, actors, doctors, etc.), Tatlin's simple cut-out suit, Rodchenko's functional coverall, Burylin's and Griun's homage to engineering, were but a few of the many solutions to the problem of creating a new form of dress. For example, one group advocated nudity as the truly democratic costume and organized a series of "Evenings of the Denuded Body" in Moscow in 1922; the artist Yurii Annenkov liked the idea of throwaway paper clothing; Exter and Yakulov favored the high-fashion, bourgeois ensemble, maintaining that the proletarian woman also had the right to be "well dressed."

In spite of their claims to the contrary, the Constructivists were an elite and sophisticated group who really had little understanding of mass taste. Lamanova's dresses were modeled by Lilia Brik (Vladimir Mayakovsky's companion) and Elsa Triolet in Paris; Popova's dresses, ultimately, hardly differed from Sonia Delaunay's expensive garments for wealthy Parisiennes; and the idea of wearing no clothing or paper clothing in the Russian winter did not evoke enthusiasm. By 1924, and especially after the 1925 Exhibition of Decorative and Industrial Arts in Paris, where the close similarities between Soviet "Communist" and Western "capitalist" textile designs were immediately manifest, new definitions of Soviet textile design arose. A direct result was the rejection of the purely geometric motif in favor of symbolic images such as the hammer and sickle, cogwheels, and factories. These designs — illustrated here — acquired greater popularity than the purely abstract ones and were reproduced at mills all over the Soviet Union. They served at once as propaganda for the ongoing industrialization of the country, especially during the time of the First Five Year Plan, and as cheerful, dynamic designs that had immediate meaning for the workers and peasants.

This move toward a more narrative or thematic textile and clothing design paralleled the general orientation of Soviet culture in the late 1920s and 1930s to traditional, accessible styles. At first glance, these eulogies of technology, sports, transportation, and so on might seem to be more representative of the social and political aims of the young Soviet state, but if we stop to think, we might wonder how American tractors in bucolic rococo settings or Art Deco light bulbs looking like details from the Chrysler Building in New York City were any more Soviet or Communist than the Constructivist projects. Moreover, the meaning of the Red Army or Navy themes is lost as soon as the material is folded into a head scarf; and the noble symbology of the hammer and sickle is lost if you sit on it. The critic David Arkin lamented this in his survey of Soviet textiles in 1929: "An extreme abundance of very old designs and a breach between the designs and the form of dress are most characteristic of the entire artistic side of our textile industry."[7] But thanks precisely to this breach we can now disregard the original purpose of these textile designs and appreciate them for their color, their rhythm, their charming anachronism. In spite of Stepanova's impassioned words, we perceive them as "works of art."

John E. Bowlt

Notes

1. Varst (V. Stepanova): "Kostium segodniashnego dnia — prozodezhda" in *Lef*, Moscow, 1923, No. 2, April-May, p. 65.
2. Alexei Gan: *Konstruktivizm*, Tver, 1922. English translation in John E. Bowlt (ed.): *Russian Art of the Avant-Garde: Theory and Criticism 1902-1934*, New York: Viking, p. 221.
3. The decree was first published in *Izvestiia VTsIK*, Moscow, 1918, 14 April. reprinted in I. Grabar et al. (eds.): *Istoriia russkogo iskusstva*, Moscow: Academy of Sciences of the USSR, 1957, Vol. 11, p. 25.
4. The best source of information and illustrations on this subject is A. Galushkina et al. (eds.): *Agitatsionno-massovoe iskusstvo pervykh let Oktiabria*, Moscow: Iskusstvo, 1971.
5. A. Blok: "Dvenadtsat" (1918) in V. Orlov (ed.): *Alexandr Blok: Sochineniia v odnom tome*, Moscow-Leningrad: State Publishing House for Creative Literature, 1946, p. 257.
6. N. Tarabukin: *Ot molberta k mashine*, Moscow: Rabotnik prosveshcheniia, 1923, pp. 23-24.
7. D. Arkin: "Iskusstvo veshchi" in *Ezhegodnik literatury i iskusstva na 1929*, Moscow: Communist Academy, 1929, p. 450.

The first ten years that followed the October Revolution saw a prodigious development of the art of propaganda. The need to educate the people in the ideas and conquests of October gave rise to Lenin's plan for propaganda in the form of monumental decoration in streets and city squares, mass spectacles, and poetry composed on the occasion of the revolution's most significant anniversaries. Textiles also became a form of propaganda, together with political posters, graphics, and even porcelains.

The twenties and the beginning of the thirties represent a particularly interesting moment in the history of the Soviet textile industry. Cotton prints of this period, produced by mills in Moscow and its outskirts, in Leningrad, Slisselburg, Ivanovo and Serpuchovo, display a diversified panorama. On the one hand, there are Ivanovo's sateens and cotton prints with traditional pink and mauve bouquets against a red background or fabrics decorated with the "cucumber" design printed in the old style, and, on the other, fabrics with "informal" designs typical of Moscow's mills. Fabrics also imitated jacquard embroidery and designs, and more expensive fabrics, such as Karabanovo's gay cottons, were dyed with alizarin and used motifs from the old folk traditions and even more complicated designs. At the same time, fabrics were being produced of lightweight materials with almost no decoration.

Within this range, so varied in both quality and esthetic choice, fabrics

Petrograd, 1917

with propagandistic designs and on "new themes" — as they were then called — are particularly notable. The originality of these artistic studies and their innovative esthetic solutions make this sector of the textile industry especially interesting.

The rare, modest fabrics preserved in the Russian State Museum and the museums of Moscow, Zagorsk, Serpuchovo, and Ivanovo — those cottons, flannels, and sateens with decorations of the first Soviet symbols, the hammer and sickle, the red stars, the tools used in everyday and industrial work, compositions derived from folklore, and others reflecting the events of the postrevolutionary decade — are moving because of their immediate, direct response to questions of the moment. They spring from the desire of many artists to express, by means of fabrics, the atmosphere of mobilization common to that period, introducing into the daily life of the people an echo of revolutionary transformation, and in some way making fabric designs express the ideas of the revolution.

Decorative motifs offered, in various forms, themes which were popular during those years: "The Demonstration," "The Tractor," "Electrification," "The Struggle Against Illiteracy," "Pioneers," and "Factories." Many fabrics of this type have been preserved. Most of the designs reproduced in this volume come from the collection of the Russian State Museum in Leningrad. This collection was begun in 1931 through the efforts of I.V. Ginzburg, a specialist at the museum. It constituted the initial part of the Soviet Industrial Art Exhibit which was held in the museum at the end of 1931 and which was organized with the participation of the artists M.A. Grigoriev and N.M. Suetin. Its purpose was to present as com-

Rodchenko and Stepanova, about 1920

8

plete a picture as possible on both the productive and creative levels.

In this collection textiles coming from the mills in Ivanovo and Moscow predominated. Much less well known are the cloths produced in the Vera Slutskaya mills in Leningrad and in the Piotr Alexeyev mills in Slisselburg. The latter were destroyed during the great Civil War and now no longer exist. In fact, fabrics which testify to the activity of the Leningrad artists during the twenties and thirties are extremely rare.

The designs in the Soviet Textile Industry Exhibit that had opened in Moscow in 1923 were displayed — in 1931˙— in a special section and belong only to the early twenties, years which coincide with a difficult period for the textile industry. Initially, in September 1920 the large plant set up at Ivanovo-Voznesensk was opened, and in October the Susnevkil plant. That same year the Treckgornaya mill in Moscow began operations again. At the beginning of 1921 the textile union counted 398 mills in the country, of which 286 were in operation. During the years of the economic crisis brought about by civil war and foreign intervention, the mills and factories — due to the scarcity of raw materials, skilled labor, and fuel — underwent a process not only of stagnation but actually of slow ruin. It appeared that hunger and the crisis would in the long run finish them off, yet despite these difficulties, towards the end of the twenties production was resumed in a number of mills — at Sui, Serpuchovo, Kinesma, Ivanovo, and Moscow.

Given these circumstances, it is clear that the artistic sector of production was not of a very high order. The textiles produced in that period, very small in quantity when compared to the needs of a population living through the hardships of the civil war, were quite simple, with printed decorations based on old patterns that required only a very elementary manufacturing process. The textile industry attained a more stable footing in 1923. As a consequence, the textile mills were able to participate in the Pan-Russian Artistic Products Exhibit, which opened in March 1923, and the Pan-Russian Agricultural Exhibit, where a special textile pavilion was set up. "This exhibit," a weavers' newspaper commented, "is the first in the world which does not have commercial and advertising aims. Our exhibit provides material for thought and study."

Participants in the Pan-Russian Exhibition included such well-known artists as V. Muchina and A. Exter, contributors in those days to *Fashion Atelier*. This magazine, founded in Moscow at the beginning of 1923, had as its goal the creation of a new kind of modern dress which would correspond to the exigencies of the new forms of Soviet life. "The rhythm of modern life," Exter wrote, "demands a minimum loss of time and energy. To present-day fashions which change according to the whims of the merchants, we must counterpose a way of dressing that is functional and beautiful in its simplicity . . ." (T. Strizenova, in *Decorative Art in the USSR*, 1967, no. 1, p. 31). That same year *Fashion Atelier* began publishing an illustrated magazine whose contributors, together with

Exter and Muchina, included the artists S. Cechonin, B. Kustodiev, K. Juon, and K. Petrov-Vodkin. In this magazine there was no talk of a new kind of cloth, yet it goes without saying that a new type of dress was unthinkable without a new type of textile decoration. In fact, the publication of *Fashion Atelier* did not get beyond its first number. Yet this one issue showed how already at the beginning of the twenties, when the So-

Rodchenko, "Champions, England and France," watercolor and ink, 1919

viet textile industry was barely overcoming the crisis, the people involved were concerned with the esthetic nature of their products. This is also shown in an article that appeared at the beginning of 1923 in *Pravda*, urging artists to deal with industrial problems. The first artists to respond to this appeal were L. Popova, V. Stepanova, A. Rodchenko, and A. Exter, who sent their sketches to the first mill which made cotton prints in Moscow. They were young artists, pioneers, enthusiastic about industrial art, fascinated by the problems of artistic construction, and impelled by the romantic dream of making art a part of the people's daily life.

"Cotton cloth is a product of artistic culture just as much as a painting; there is no reason to distinguish one from the other," the art critic J. Tugencholyed wrote. "In the textile field, instead of the previous old imitations of foreign models, we have new fabric designs created by young artists under the guidance of L. Popova, designs in which for the first time the research of artists on the Left has been applied to the industry; they reflect all the intense dynamic of life" (E. Murina in *Decorative Art in the USSR*, 1967, no. 8, p. 24). They were easy to produce, modern in style, and printed in large quantities. F. Roginskaya, the art historian, described these textile designs executed by the Constructivists as "the first

The group Unisov, Vitebsk, 1920: Ermolaeva, Malevich, Tchichimik, El Lissitzky

An agit-prop group painting a railroad car

Soviet fashion" (F. Roginskaya, *Soviet Textile Industry*, 1930, p. 36).

Alongside the work of the Constructivists, there were other schools of textile design. There were fabrics with subjects whose ornamental design recalled the surrounding world. The very titles of these subjects — "October," "Collectivization," "Flying Squads," "The Factory," "Industry," "Building Construction" — prove that they were directly connected with daily life. These designs, produced by many mills and sold in the most remote corners of the Soviet Republic, played an important role in propaganda and in support of socialist ideas. They celebrated the first Five-Year Plan, the Oriental peoples' awakening to a new way of life, and the struggle against illiteracy. In these designs one can feel the pulse of the times, the intense activity of a country transformed by the October Revolution. Unlike the textile designs of the Constructivists, which critics described as "abstract" or "geometric," these works were called "thematic" or "propaganda" patterns. When they were put on the market or shown at exhibits, they provoked heated debates. Articles by O. Brik, N. Poluek-tovaya, F. Roginskaya, and others published in the periodical press remind us of the lively polemic atmosphere of those years. Between 1927 and 1931 "thematic" designs predominated. They were created and popularized by such textile artists as L. Silich, O. Fedoseyeva, D. Preobraz-henskaya, M. Chvostenko, F. Antonova, M. Nazarevskaya, and L. Rait-sev, all graduates of VCHUTEIN (Textile Faculty of the Institute of Arts and Industrial Design), and by old local designers such as S. Burylin and V. Maslov, experts in production. The Textile Section of the Youth Union in the Association of Artists of the Revolution, whose founders were the artists M. Nazarevskaya, L. Raitsev, and F. Roginskaya, played an active part in the wide-scale distribution of these new designs.

Thematic designs varied greatly. Some reproduced mechanically the old compositions of the past, while others proposed new motifs. One of the most characteristic was the sateen "Tractor," widely distributed in those times, devised by the Ivanovo artist V. Maslov, the first example of this new kind of design. The theme, which symbolized the life of a Soviet village, was very popular in those years and was used in many variations. In Maslov's design, against a light blue-gray background, large figurative factory trademarks are framed by bunches of berries, fruits, and dark green leaves. In the free spaces are scenes of agricultural work. A

Rodchenko, illustration from the magazine *Lef*

type of decorative composition which goes back to the French silks of the seventeenth and eighteenth centuries could also be seen among the national textiles. Maslov introduced into this old compositional scheme a more up-to-date theme, combining narrative design with elementary symbology, fused together by graphic style and a luminous color range, according to the tradition of the Ivanovo mills. The richness of

Banners on the old Marinsky Palace (above) and the panel "Birth of the New World" (below)

color in these cloths, its difficulty of execution, which requires a series of complicated printing procedures, make it clearly superior to other cloths produced during those years, which were made with only one or two rollers. Probably the fabric was executed as a design to be exhibited; in fact, at the Moscow Soviet Textile Industry exhibit, which opened in 1928, it was presented as a prototype for possible textile production.

Some of the cloth produced in the large mill at Ivanovo-Voznesensk is similar in both subject and composition to the "Tractor" fabric. It does not have a particular name. The fact that the idea of a narrative pattern, the composition, and the entire design are treated in a similar fashion leads one to think that its creator may be Maslov. Unfortunately, our information about this artist is meager. We know that he worked in the mill at Teikov, but his designs apparently were not printed in Teikov alone.

In the spirit of the traditional Ivanovo fabrics, unknown artists produced a series of dress materials printed with bright-color roses surrounded by airplanes that remind us of the traditional *millefleurs*. Despite their conventionality, these works are distinguished by their highly decorative and festive air, characteristic of traditional Russian decoration.

Once again these examples indicate the difficult conditions under which textile artists of the twenties functioned in their search for new

Varvara Stepanova (second from right) with students from the Vchutemas, about 1920

Rodchenko, drawings for an overall (1921), teapot (1922), and lamp (1929)

images of everyday life. Some of these works show precise and original artistic solutions. This is the case of the sateens with decorations on the theme "Work to Transform the Countryside." In these instances, as in the tractor fabric, traditional criteria typical of the old brocades are used. Nevertheless, here the theme is used only as a pretext for compositions that are in themselves much more interesting and resolved at a level of abstraction and stylization.

In one case, the decoration inserted on broad stripes coincides with the weft of the cloth, which acts as a decorative background element. This relationship and the compositional stylization of the details — tractors, people, sheaves of wheat — render the whole barely perceptible from a distance. The composition acquires a particularly intense energy from the contrast of the groupings, and from the rhythmical succession of colors, orange, blue, and pink. The author is unknown, although the oldest artists of the Ivanovo mill tend to think that this is the work of Sergei Petrovich Burylin, a well-known designer, the author of many textile designs.

Burylin (1876 - 1942), together with Popova and Stepanova, should be regarded as one of the pioneers of Soviet textile art. Among the Ivanovo textile artists whose work has made the fabrics of this city famous, he occupies an important place as an innovator of textile design. "His work belongs to the great and original school of Ivanovo fabrics" — so his colleague S. Loginov described Burylin (in *Workers World*, 1967). Burylin's compositional designs express a special virtuosity. They are elegant classical etchings against a black background, or blue caps with red stars combined harmoniously with images of fish and fishermen's nets, or light cotton prints for dresses with decorations of mechanical gears or stacks of wheat. Burylin's fabrics with minute designs in the form of ears of wheat, five-pointed stars, and hammers and sickles were shown at the Universal Exposition in Paris in 1925 and won the gold medal. The son of an illustrator, Burylin had no professional artistic education, yet he knew perfectly all the coloring and composition criteria required by factory production. His school was the factory. Observing the variety of his fabrics, one notices that the new themes, although not always carried out successfully, did not daunt the artist. His work testifies to the fact that uppermost in the minds of all these artists was the need to create a new textile style.

In one series of fabrics some artists attempted to portray the conquests of the first Five-Year Plan, the new style of Soviet life, and the dynamic rhythm and beauty of industrial processes. This series, whose composition represented stylized details of industrial elements, was described as "Designs of Production". A typical example is the fabric designed by the artist R. Matveyeva of the great Ivanovo-Voznesensk plant. It is a dress fabric whose compositional elements are based on the rhythmic repetition of the objects tied to production: sickle, hammer, black outlines of gear wheels. The details, felicitously harmonized with a series of colors, meet the specific requirements of textile decoration.

The floral decoration typical of foreign bourgeois taste in the thirties was supplanted by thematic designs, industrial motifs, or related patterns which describe events that had become recurrent after the October Revolution. Quite common are textiles on themes such as "Electrifi-

Porcelain

cation," "Building," and "The Work and Customs of Oriental Peoples." This last theme especially was developed in a series of variations preserving the stylistic elements of Oriental textiles. A further development is recorded in 1930, when many artists who had graduated from VCHUTEIN, such as E. Lapsinaya and O. Fedoseyeva, who worked on the themes of "Aviation" and "Tractors," joined the Ivanovo mills. With very simple means — for example, the well-known dotted design with a red outline produced with a single roller — the artist was able to transform a simple functional cloth into a work of art.

An interesting series of thematic designs is tied to the name of O. Bogoslovskaya, graduated in 1929 from the Artistic Industrial Institute, who worked at first in the Sosnev mill and later in the mill in Ivanovo which bears the name of the worker F. Zinoviev. Her "Electrification" design on Indian cloth is particularly original and represents a successful combination of the qualities of the cloth with elements of novelty. The proportions of the design of the light bulb, with rays of light, and the color combine in a free association with a floral decoration, a recurrent characteristic of this artist. In watercolor sketches donated by the artist to the Russian Museum in 1972, her great love of color is evident and the painterly principle typical also of her later work predominates.

Cup and saucer

A special contribution to fabric design was made at the end of the twenties by O.P. Griun, an artist in the mill at Treckgornaya and one of the teachers at VCHUTEIN. His designs are extremely personal and most unusual. Usually Griun included in the composition various details connected with textile production, such as spools and other instruments. The choice of color, the precise proportions of the design, the manner in which it was deployed across the surface, point to an artist of great talent. He had particular success with a fabric painted with Soviet emblems and a representation of the world surrounded by the rays of the sun. The arrangement of these elements, the precision of the design, perceptible even at a distance, and the color contrasts evoked considerable emotional response. The romantic enthusiasm of the basic idea, its symbolic meaning, show us the feeling that infused those ten post-revolutionary years.

Preobrazhenskaya's works for the Ivanovo and Moscow mills offer further examples of fresh originality. They are fabrics on the subjects of "Swimmers" and "The Eighth of March," among others. Her flannel print of "Swimmers" is outstanding because of the skill with which the theme is stylized by the repetition of agile silhouettes. The "Eighth of March" design has a wide gamut of pink tones which in the distribution of the de-

Nina Kogan, gouache, about 1930

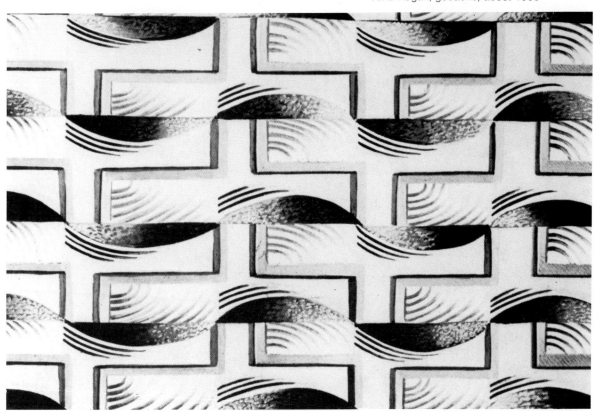

Varvara Stepanova, photograph by Rodchenko, about 1925

sign recalls the traditional curtains that were once popular among the peasants. However, the dynamic solution of the compositions and the festive quality of the subject make this fabric very "modern" for those years.

One of the most talented graduates of the VCHUTEIN was L. Silich, whose diploma design, a dress fabric called "The Reaper" or "The Peasant," executed according to the old piquet technique (extremely thin white lines on a colored background) is striking because of its elegant simplicity and its concise and delicate stylization. The repetition of women holding sheaves of wheat imparts a flowing rhythm to the decoration.

Artists of this period had to be concerned not only with problems of an esthetic order but also with creating a design whose elements of novelty could be reproduced under conditions of mass production. Kerchiefs such as "Airplanes" and "Collectivization," by Fedoseyeva, and "The Rye" by Bobysev, belong to the series executed on rollers. Limited production possibilities and the great demand for fabrics compelled the artists to economize as much as possible on artistic means. This explains in part the vast spread of designs executed on a single roller during the years 1927 - 1929, in which the background color of the material is an integrating part of the design. Within the limitations of a single color - red, black, dark blue - together with the basic background, the artists were able to achieve an exceptional decorative expressiveness. It is enough to cite such prints as Burylin's "Tractor," Matveyeva's "Water Sports," Preobrazhenskaya's "Transportation," and Raitsev's "Demonstration."

Different in color, execution, number of rollers used, and variety of ornamental elements are the fabrics produced on commission for specific celebrations. The design of the fabric executed in 1933 by Raitsev, "Mechanization of the Red Army," celebrating the fifteenth anniversary of the Red Army, has a particularly solemn and monumental aspect, just as the cotton print by P. Leonov with images of factories, airplanes, and sunbeams is brilliantly festive. The problems and exigencies of textile design during the period under examination are many and diverse. We have seen certain cases where the subject represented for the artist a kind of canvas on which to elaborate an ornamental design which, although recalling the chosen theme by association, did not illustrate it — in other words, cases in which the theme is subordinate to the specificity of the textile design. In others, however, the narrative principle was predominant and the fabric became a way of illustrating a particular subject. In the twenties and thirties there were many examples of the latter, as is shown in the case of Maslov, creator of the famous "Tractor" fabric and another cotton print on the theme of "Collectivization." Maslov not only uses several rollers but also adopts the technique of fading, which imitates a painter's brush strokes, perspective, and volume, and includes in

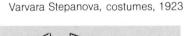

Varvara Stepanova, costumes, 1923

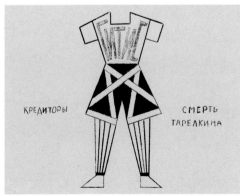

Liubov Popova, textile design (left and right), dress design (center), 1923-24

the design the text, "Society of Rural Consumption." The whole, together with the narrative subject of the scenes, gives one the impression of being confronted by a work done on an easel. The incompatibility between the nature of the cloth and these decorative methods was even more evident when the design was meant for a dress fabric. Examples of such contrast between the artist's idea and the final use of a particular cloth are numerous, and once again prove how complex was the path chosen by the artists in their search for an ornamental design in harmony with the times. Their desire to be as persuasive as possible in the choice of new subjects often forced them to scale down their ideas and to use on fabrics esthetic elements that were typical of the poster, easel painting, and publishing graphics.

The fabrics produced during the twenties present us with a complex if

Varvara Stepanova and Liubov Popova, textile designs

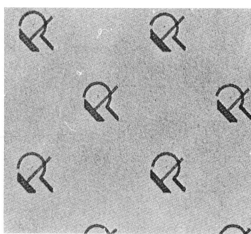

not contradictory panorama. It was a passing moment and, as was shown by the subsequent development of textile design, it was unrepeatable from the historic point of view. During the thirties there arose a renewed interest in floral decoration, which responded to new esthetic problems. Just as important are the works of those artists who strove to create a new Soviet style in textiles, a style which, without any kinship to others, would represent the characteristic traits of the epoch. These works offer us the possibility of perceiving directly the unique atmosphere of those years. Thus they preserve their fascination and their value not only for scholars of the subject, but also for those artists who are active in this field today.

I. Yasinskaya

Alexandra Exter, 1923

SOSNEV AMALGAMATED MILLS

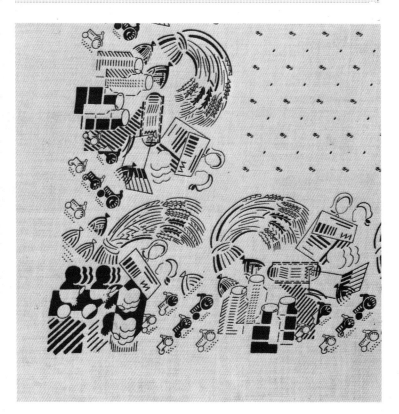

"The Collectivization"
Cotton print
1928-1930s
Fragment of a kerchief
Designed by O. Fedoseyeva
Russian Museum, Leningrad
Acquired in 1931.

facing page:
Cotton print
Late 1920s-early 1930s
Designer unknown
The I. Yasinskaya Collection,
Leningrad.

"Aquatic Sports"
Cotton print
1928-1930s
Designed by E. Lapshina
Russian Museum, Leningrad
Acquired in 1931.

Cotton print
Late 1920s-early 1930s
Designed by S. Burylin (?)
The I. Yasinskaya Collection,
Leningrad.

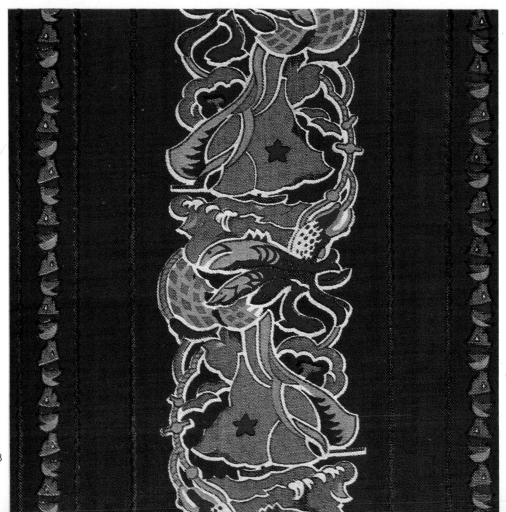

"Waste Utilization"
Cotton print
Late 1920s-early 1930s
Designer unknown
Russian Museum, Leningrad
Acquired in 1931.

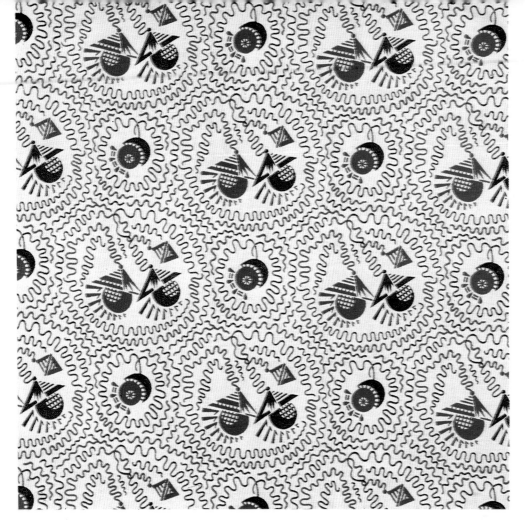

"Electric Bulbs"
Cotton print
1928-1930s
Designed by E. Lapshina
Russian Museum, Leningrad
Acquired in 1931.

"The Turkestan-Siberia Railroad"
Cotton print for the
Soviet Republics of Central Asia
1927-1930
Designer unknown
Russian Museum, Leningrad.

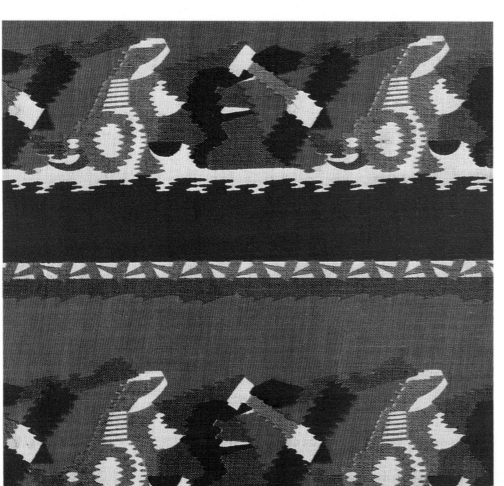

"Construction Site"
Cotton print
1920-1930
Designed by O. Bogoslovskaya (?)
Russian Museum, Leningrad
Acquired in 1931.

Cotton print
For the Soviet Republics of
Central Asia
Late 1920s-early 1930s
Designer unknown
Russian Museum, Leningrad
Acquired in 1931.

Cotton print
Late 1920s-early 1930s
Designed by S. Burylin (?)
The I. Yasinskaya Collection,
Leningrad.

facing page:
"Electric Bulbs"
Cotton print for the Soviet
Republics of Central Asia
1928-1930s
Designed by S. Strusevich
Russian Museum, Leningrad
Acquired in 1931.

Cotton print
Late 1920s-early 1930s
Designed by S. Burylin (?)
The I. Yasinskaya Collection,
Leningrad.

Cotton print
Late 1920s-early 1930s
Designer unknown
The I. Yasinskaya Collection,
Leningrad.

**"Fifteenth Anniversary
of the USSR"**
Cotton print
Early 1930s
Designed by O. Bogoslovskaya (?)
The I. Yasinskaya Collection,
Leningrad.

"Electrification"
Cotton print
Early 1930s
Designed by O. Bogoslovskaya
The I. Yasinskaya Collection,
Leningrad.

Cotton print
Industrial motif
Late 1920s-early 1930s
Designed by S. Burylin (?)
The I. Yasinskaya Collection,
Leningrad.

IVANOVO - VOZNESENSK MILLS

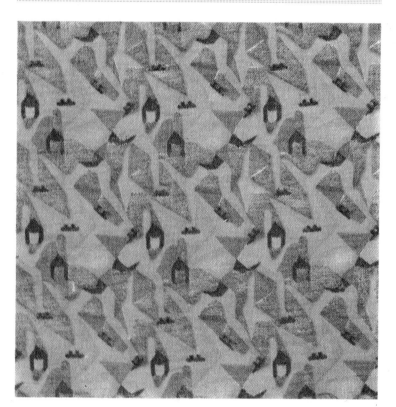

"Skaters"
Flannel
Late 1920s-early 1930s
Designed by D. Preobrazhenskaya
Russian Museum, Leningrad
Acquired in 1931.

facing page:
Cotton print
1924-early 1930s
Designer unknown
Russian Museum, Leningrad
Acquired in 1931.

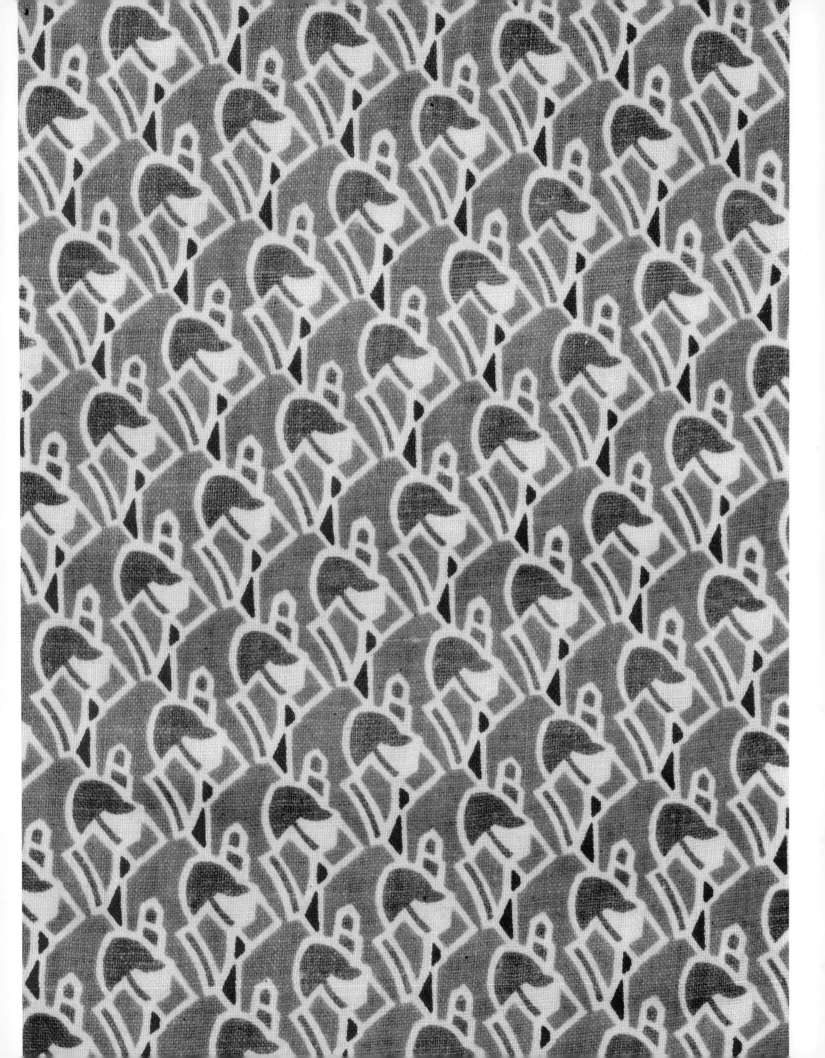

"Transport"
Cotton print
1927
Designed by D. Preobrazhenskaya
Russian Museum, Leningrad
Acquired in 1931.

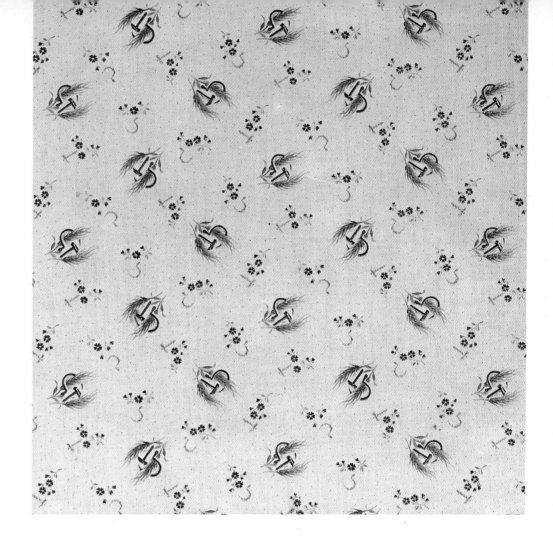

Cotton print
1924-1925
Designed by S. Burylin
Russian Museum, Leningrad
Acquired in 1931.

Cotton print
1924-1925
Designed by S. Burylin
Russian Museum, Leningrad
Acquired in 1931.

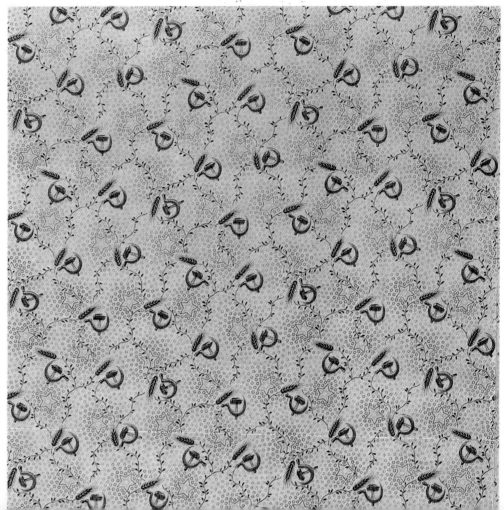

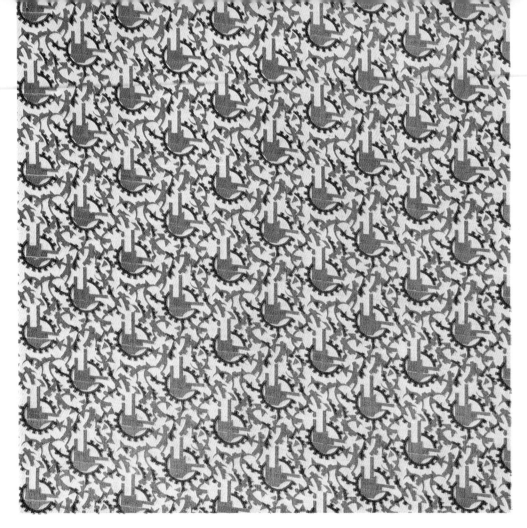

"Industry"
Cotton print
1929
Designed by R. Matveyeva
Russian Museum, Leningrad
Acquired in 1931.

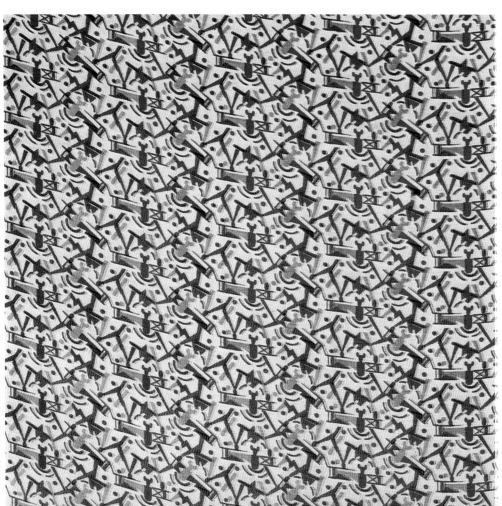

Cotton print
1927
Designed by R. Matveyeva
Russian Museum, Leningrad
Acquired in 1931.

Crepe
1927
Designed by S. Burylin
Russian Museum, Leningrad
Acquired in 1931.

"Industry"
Crepe
1930
Designed by S. Burylin
Russian Museum, Leningrad
Acquired in 1931.

"Industry"
Cotton print
1930
Designed by D. Preobrazhenskaya
Russian Museum, Leningrad
Acquired in 1931.

facing page:
Armure
1927
Designed by A. Medvedev
Russian Museum, Leningrad
Acquired in 1931.

"Factory"
Cotton print
1927
Designed by S. Burylin
Russian Museum, Leningrad
Acquired in 1931.

Decorative cotton print
1927
Designed by P. Leonov
Russian Museum, Leningrad
Acquired in 1931.

facing page:
Armure
1927
Designed by S. Burylin
Russian Museum, Leningrad
Acquired in 1931.

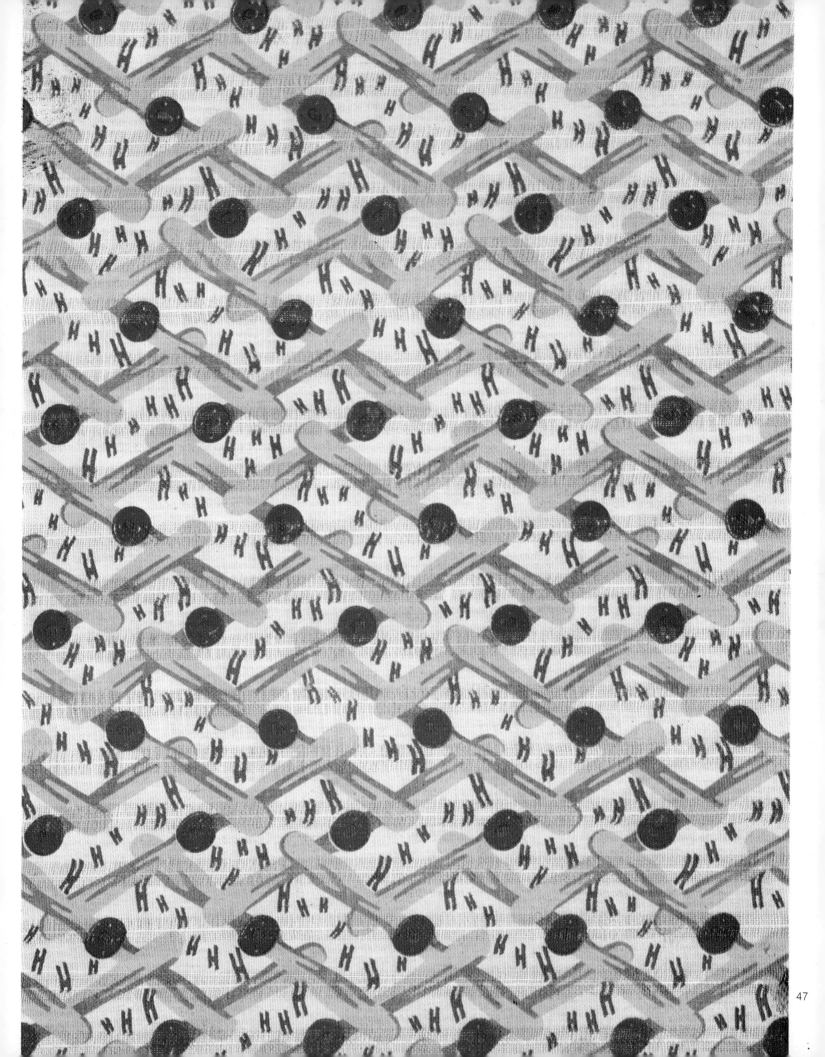

"Tractor"
Cotton print
1930
Designed by S. Burylin
Russian Museum, Leningrad
Acquired in 1931.

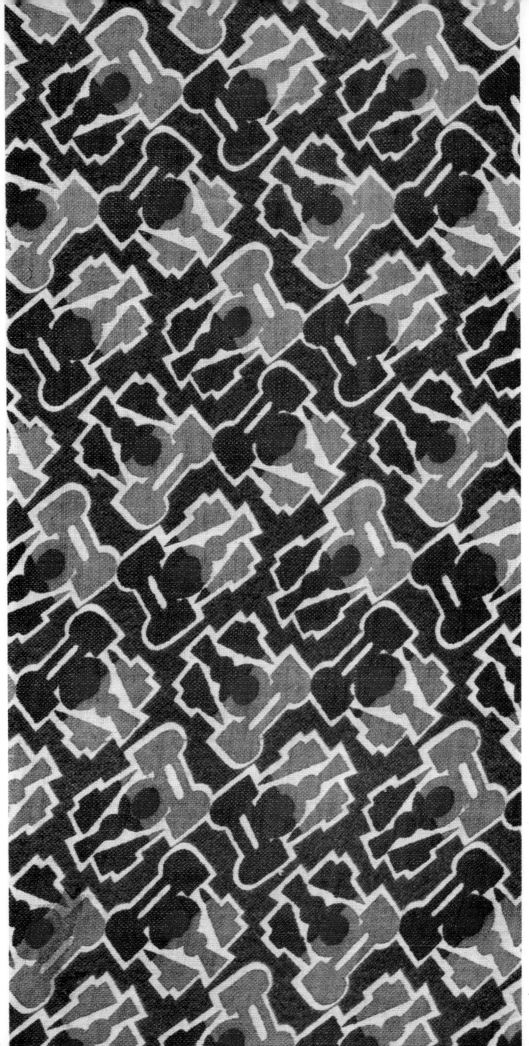

"Steam engine"
1927-1930
Designed by P. Nechvalenko
Russian Museum, Leningrad
Acquired in 1931.

"The Collectivization"
Cotton print
Late 1920s
Designed by V. Maslov (?)
The I. Yasinskaya Collection,
Leningrad.

"Tractor"
Sateen
Late 1920s
Designed by V. Maslov
Russian Museum, Leningrad
Acquired in 1931.

Armure
1927
Designed by S. Burylin
Russian Museum, Leningrad
Acquired in 1931.

"TREKHGORNAYA MANUFAKTURA" MILL

"Mechanization of the Red Army"
Sateen
1933
Designed by L. Raitser
The V. Mukhina Higher School of
Art and Design, Leningrad.

facing page:
"Young Pioneers"
Serge
Late 1920s-early 1930s
Designed by O. Griun
Russian Museum, Leningrad
Acquired in 1931.

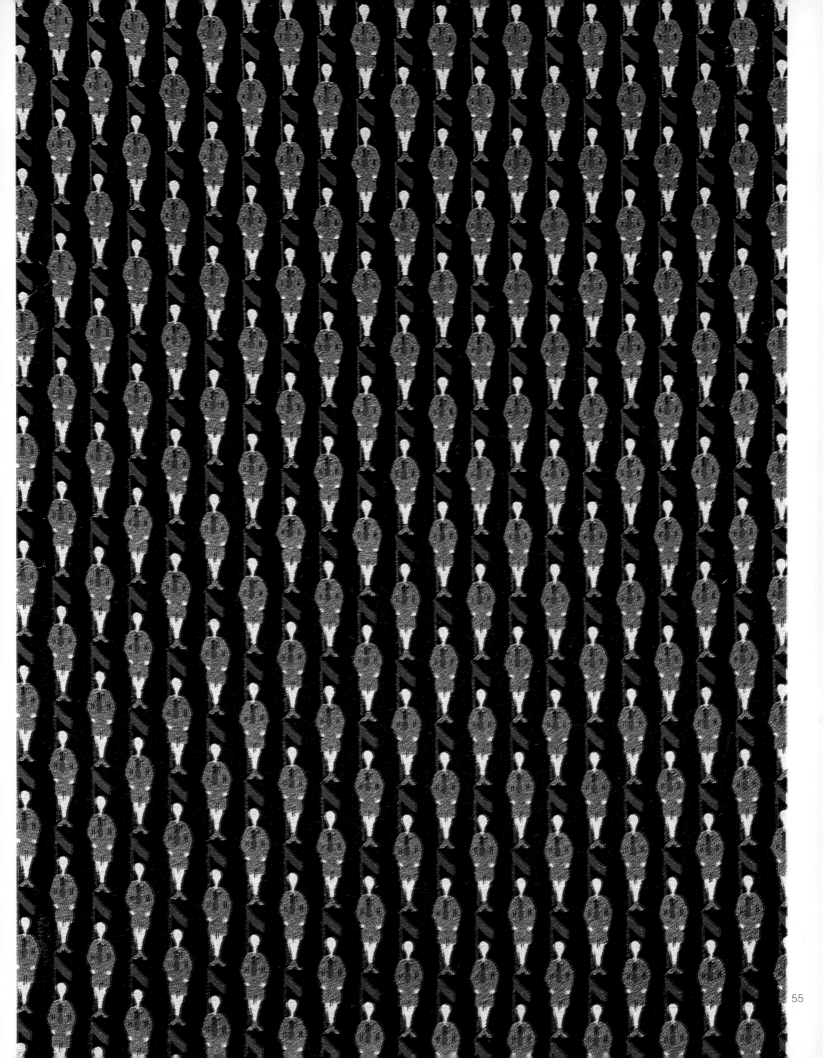

Cotton print
Late 1920s-early 1930s
Designer unknown
The I. Yasinskaya Collection,
Leningrad.

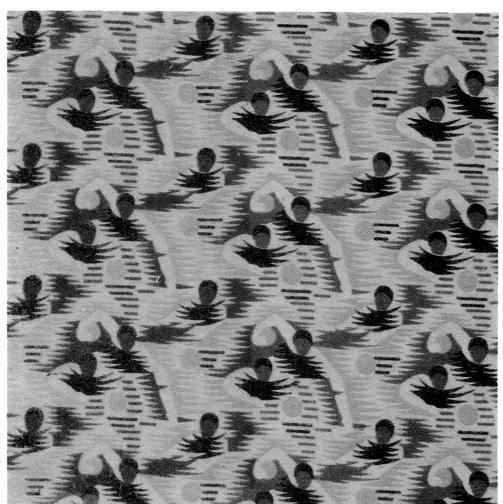

"Aquatic Sports"
Flannel
Late 1920s-early 1930s
Designed by D. Preobrazhenskaya
Russian Museum, Leningrad
Acquired in 1931.

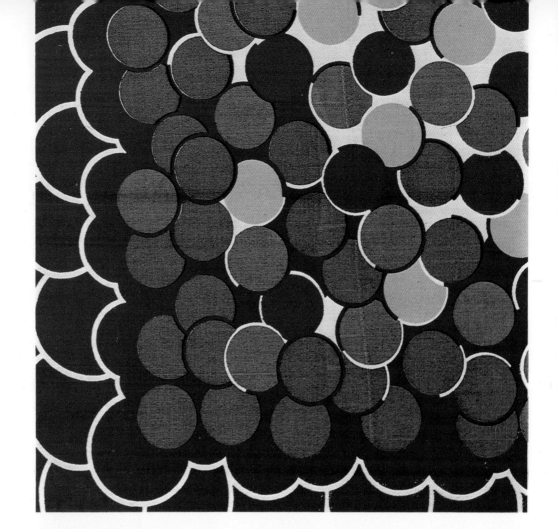

Cotton print
Late 1920s-early 1930s
Fragment of a kerchief
Designer unknown
Russian Museum, Leningrad
Acquired in 1931.

"Demonstration"
Cotton print
1929
Designed by L. Raitser
Russian Museum, Leningrad
Acquired in 1931.

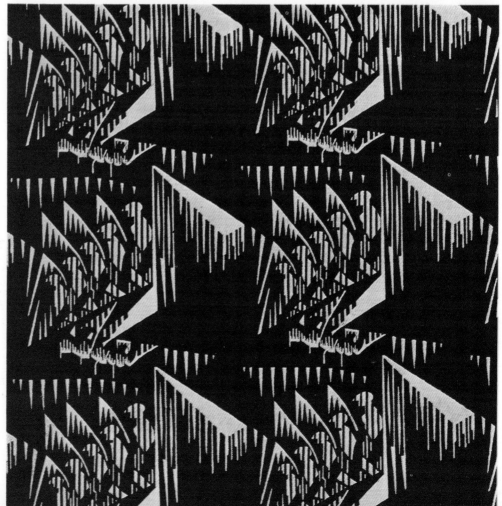

Decorative cotton print
1924-1925
Designed by O. Griun
The V. Mukhina Higher School of
Art and Design, Leningrad.

facing page:
"Mechanization of the Red Army"
Sateen
1933
Designed by L. Raitser
The I. Yasinskaya Collection,
Leningrad.

**"The Village Consumers'
Cooperative Society"**
Cotton print
Late 1920s
Designed by V. Maslov
Russian Museum, Leningrad
Acquired in 1931.

UNIDENTIFIED MILLS
from the Ivanovo collection

Decorative sateen
Early 1930s
Designed by S. Burylin (?)
Russian Museum, Leningrad
Acquired in 1931.

Decorative cotton print
Late 1920s-early 1930s
Designer unknown
Russian Museum, Leningrad
Acquired in 1931.

Cotton print
Late 1920s-early 1930s
Designer unknown
The I. Yasinskaya Collection,
Leningrad.

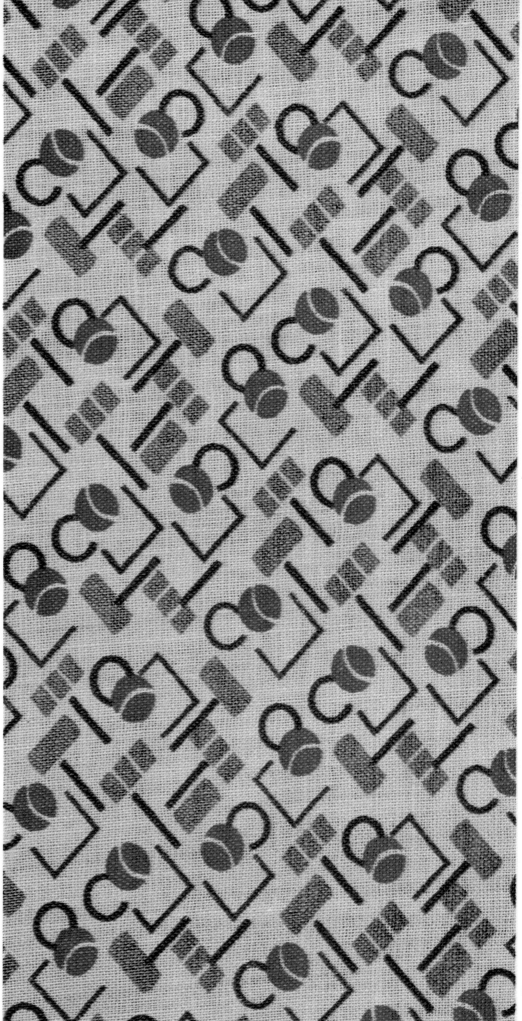

Decorative sateen
Late 1920s-early 1930s
Designer unknown
Russian Museum, Leningrad
Acquired in 1931.

facing page:
"Reaping Women"
Cotton print
Late 1920s-early 1930s
Designed by L. Silich
Russian Museum, Leningrad
Acquired in 1931.

Cotton print
Late 1920s-early 1930s
Designer unknown
The I. Yasinskaya Collection,
Leningrad.

Cotton print
Late 1920s-early 1930s
Designer unknown
Russian Museum, Leningrad
Acquired in 1931.

"**March 8th** (International Women's Day)"
Cotton print
Late 1920s-early 1930s
Designed by D. Preobrazhenskaya
Russian Museum, Leningrad
Acquired in 1931.

"**Down with Illiteracy!**"
Cotton print for the Soviet Republics of Central Asia
Late 1920s-early 1930s
Designer unknown
The I. Yasinskaya Collection, Leningrad.

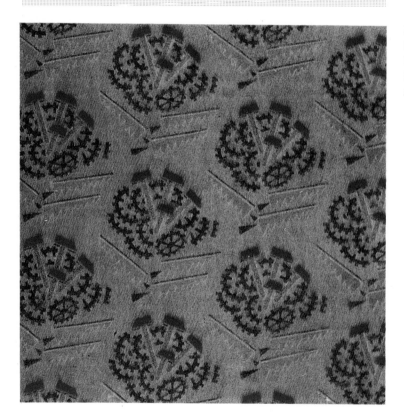

Flannel
Mid 1920s-early 1930s
Designed by S. Burylin
Russian Museum, Leningrad
Acquired in 1931.

facing page:
"Airplanes"
Cotton print
Late 1920s-early 1930s
Fragment of a kerchief
Designed by O. Fedoseyeva
Russian Museum, Leningrad
Acquired in 1931.

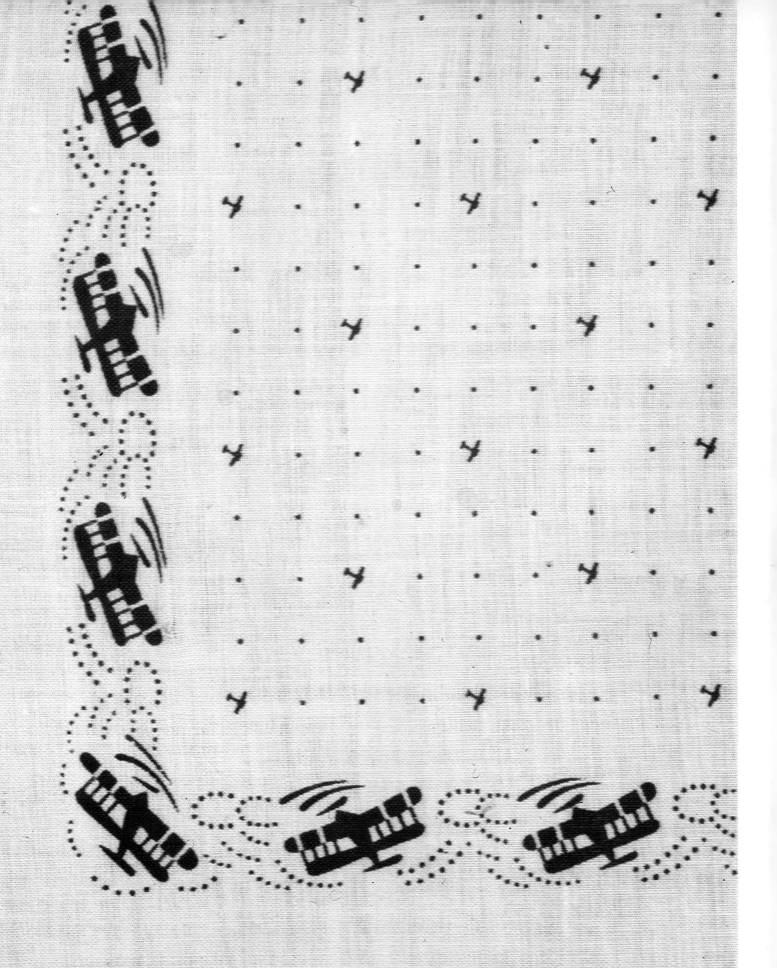

"MOPR" (International
Organization for Aid to
Champions of Revolution)
Serge
1929
Designed by D. Preobrazhenskaya
Russian Museum, Leningrad
Acquired in 1931.

Cotton print
Industrial motif
Late 1920s-early 1930s
Designed by S. Burylin
Russian Museum, Leningrad
Acquired in 1931.

Cotton print
Late 1920s-early 1930s
Designer unknown
The I. Yasinskaya Collection,
Leningrad.

Cotton print
Late 1920s-early 1930s
Designed by O. Fedoseyeva
Russian Museum, Leningrad.
Acquired in 1931.

UNIDENTIFIED MILLS

**"Daily Life of the Peoples of
the East"**
Cotton print
Late 1920s-early 1930s
Designer unknown
The V. Mukhina Higher School of
Art and Design, Leningrad.

facing page:
Cotton print
Late 1920s-early 1930s
Designer unknown
Russian Museum, Leningrad
Acquired in 1931.

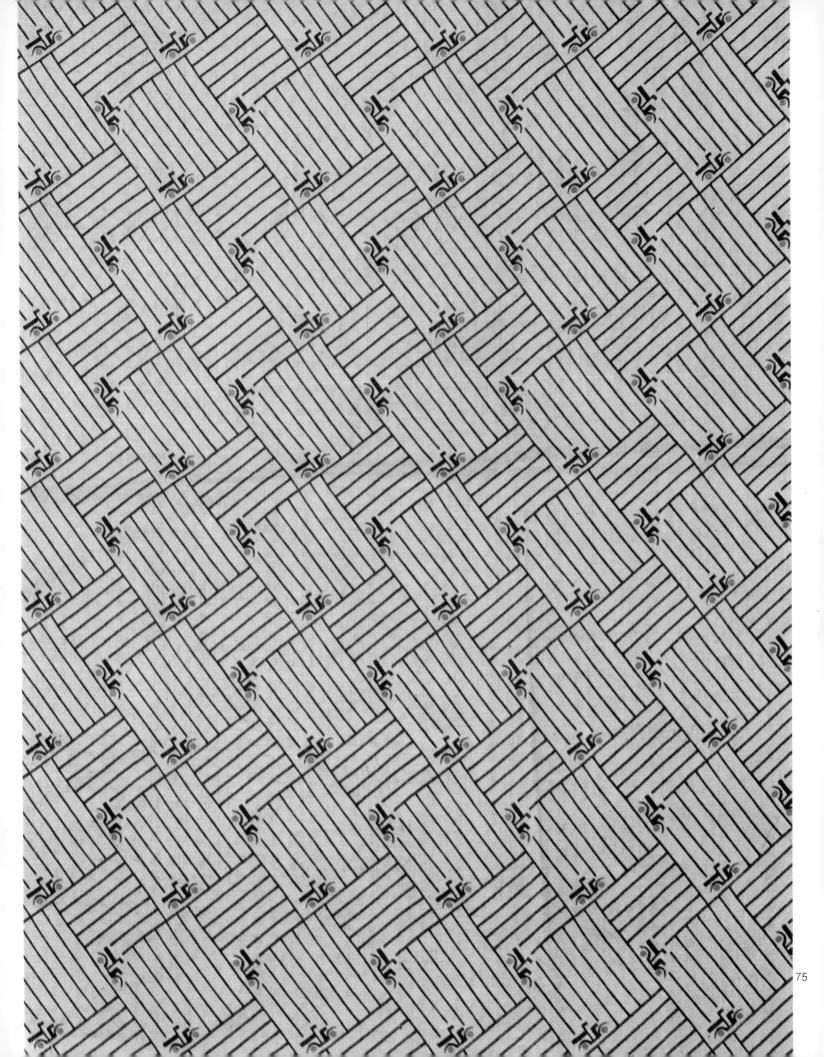

Cotton print
Late 1920s-early 1930s
Designed by M. Nazarevskaya
Russian Museum, Leningrad
Acquired in 1931.

Decorative sateen
Late 1920s-early 1930s
Designer unknown
Russian Museum, Leningrad
Acquired in 1931.

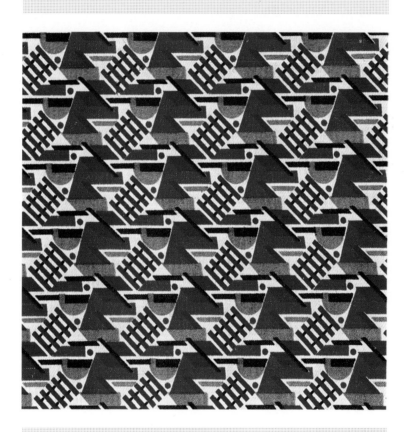

Decorative cotton print
Late 1920s-early 1930s
Designer unknown
Russian Museum, Leningrad
Acquired in 1931.

Cotton print
Late 1920s-early 1930s
Designer unknown
Russian Museum, Leningrad

facing page:
"Skaters"
Flannel
Late 1920s-early 1930s
Designed by D. Preobrazhenskaya
Russian Museum, Leningrad
Acquired in 1931.

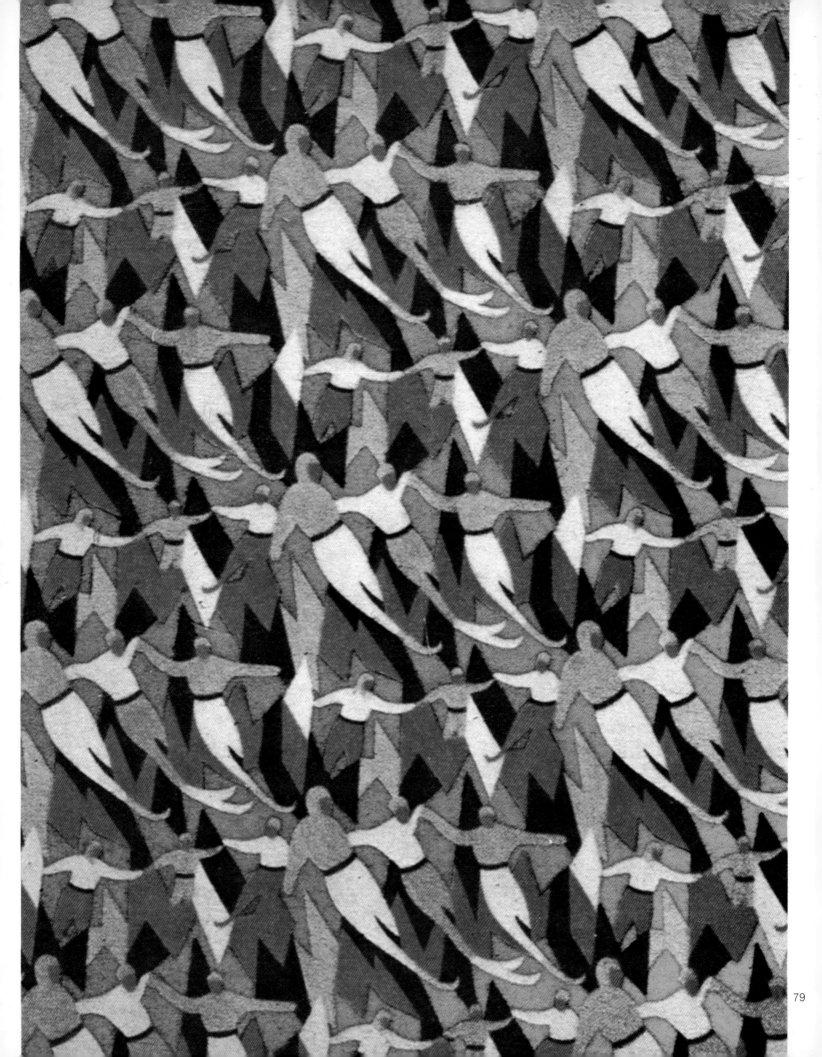

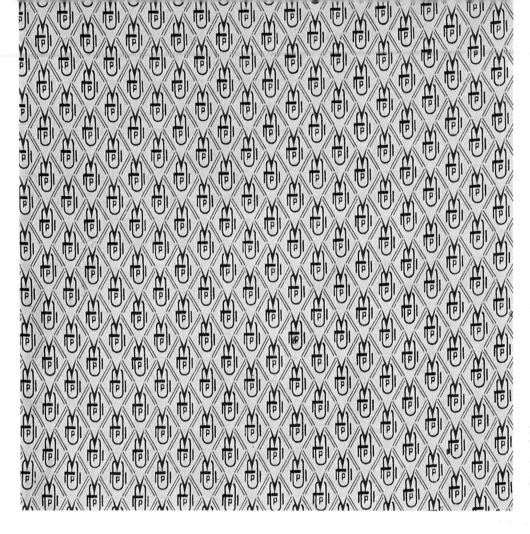

"MOPR"
(International
Organization for Aid to
Champions of Revolution)
Cotton print
1930
Designer unknown
Russian Museum, Leningrad
Acquired in 1931.

"Air Fleet"
Flannel
1930
Designed by M. Anufriyeva
Russian Museum, Leningrad
Acquired in 1931.

Flannel
Late 1920s-early 1930s
Designer unknown
Russian Museum, Leningrad
Acquired in 1931.

Armure
Late 1920s-early 1930s
Designer unknown
Russian Museum, Leningrad
Acquired in 1931.

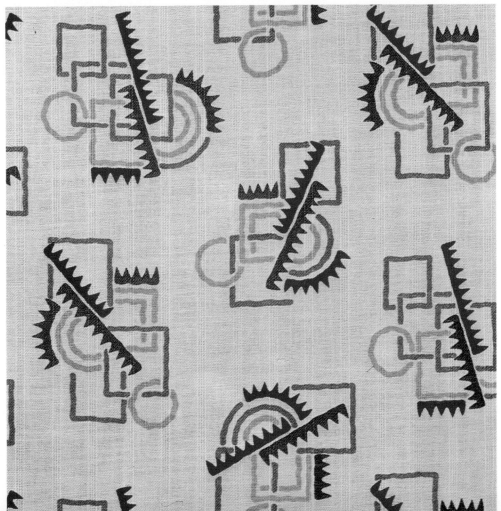

"Navy"
Sateen
Late 1920s-early 1930s
Designed by V. Lotonina
The V. Mukhina Higher School of
Art and Design, Leningrad.

facing page:
"Young Pioneers Marching"
Armure
Late 1920s-early 1930s
Designed by M. Khvostenko
Russian Museum, Leningrad
Acquired in 1931.

83

"Construction Site"
Cotton print
Late 1920s-1930s
Designed by F. Antonov
Russian Museum, Leningrad
Acquired in 1931.

Flannel
Late 1920s-early 1930s
Designer unknown
Russian Museum, Leningrad
Acquired in 1931.

Flannel
Late 1920s-early 1930s
Designer unknown
Russian Museum, Leningrad
Acquired in 1931.

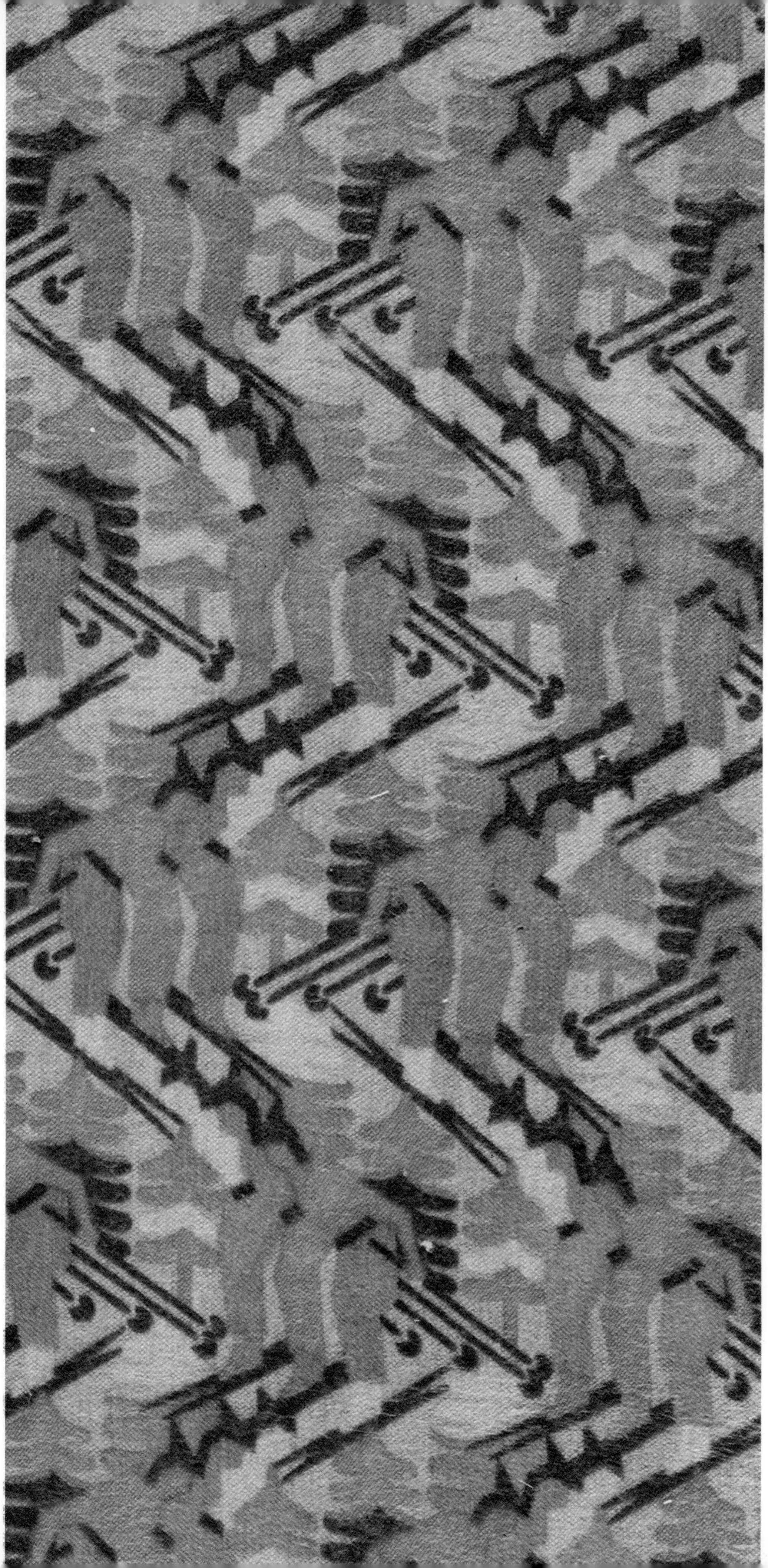

Flannel
Late 1920s-early 1930s
Designer unknown
Russian Museum, Leningrad
Acquired in 1931.

"Gathering Cotton"
Sateen
Early 1930s
Designed by M. Nazarevskaya
The I. Yasinskaya Collection,
Leningrad.

facing page:
"Hydroelectric Plant"
Flannel
Early 1930s
Designed by D. Preobrazhenskaya
The I. Yasinskaya Collection,
Leningrad.

Flannel
Late 1920s-early 1930s
Designer unknown
Russian Museum, Leningrad
Acquired in 1931.

VERA SLUTSKAYA, PIOTR ALEXEYEV, Y. SVERDLOV & FIRST COTTON-PRINTING MILLS

"The October Revolution"
Cotton print
1930
Designed by Belozemtseva
Russian Museum, Leningrad
Acquired in 1931.

facing page:
"Air Squadron"
Volta (a thin cotton fabric)
1929
Fragment of a kerchief
Designed by T. Chachkhiani
Russian Museum, Leningrad
Acquired in 1931.

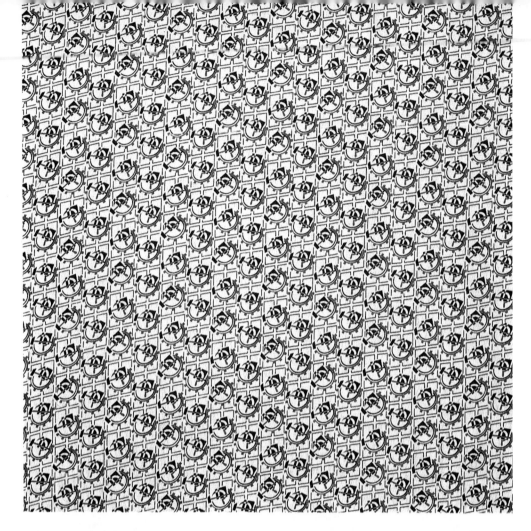

"Sickle, Hammer and Gear"
Cotton print
1930
Designer unknown
Russian Museum, Leningrad
Acquired in 1931.

"Spools"
Serge
1928
Designed by O. Griun
Russian Museum, Leningrad
Acquired in 1931.

"The USSR"
Maya (a thin cotton fabric)
Late 1920s-early 1930s
Designer unknown
Russian Museum, Leningrad
Acquired in 1931.

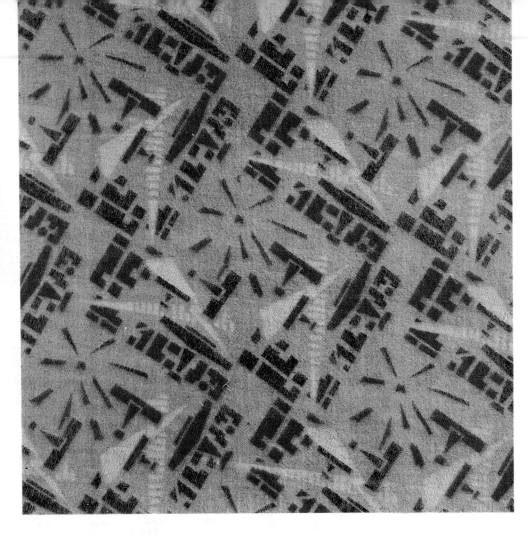

"Airplanes Flying"
Flannel
1930
Designer unknown
Russian Museum, Leningrad
Acquired in 1931.

"Tractor"
Flannel
1930
Designer unknown
Russian Museum, Leningrad
Acquired in 1931.

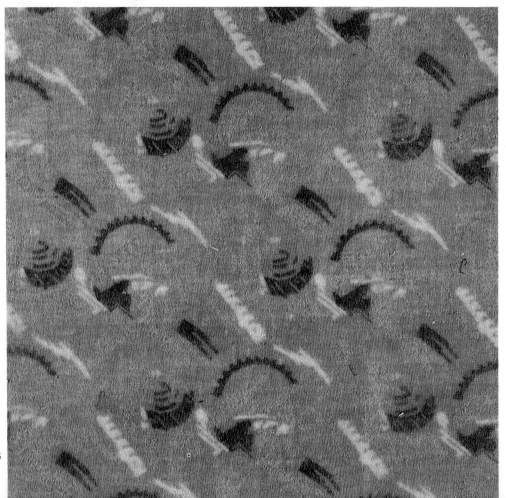

Volta
(a thin cotton fabric)
1929
Designed by E. Nikitina
Russian Museum, Leningrad
Acquired in 1931.

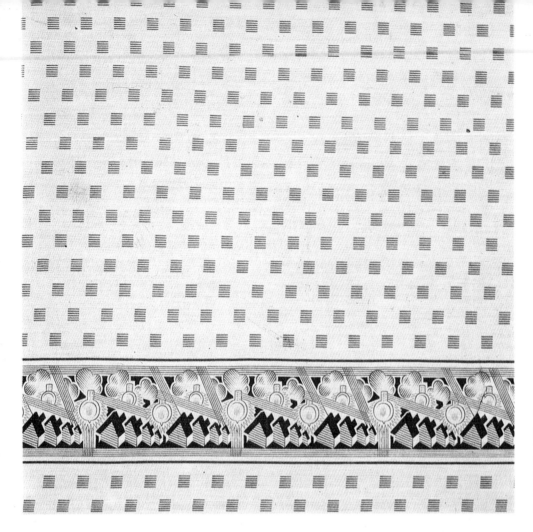

"Electrification of the Village"
Cotton print
1929
Fragment of a kerchief
Designer unknown
Russian Museum, Leningrad
Acquired in 1931.

"Red Army Man on Guard"
Flannel
1930
Designed by E. Bykov
Russian Museum, Leningrad
Acquired in 1931.

5 th OCTOBER, THIRD INTERNATIONAL,
"KRASNAYA TALKA", N. ZHIDELEV
& G. KOROLIOV MILLS

"The Turkestan-Siberia Railroad"
Cotton print
Early 1930s
Designer unknown
The I. Yasinskaya Collection,
Leningrad.

facing page:
"Aquatic Sports"
Cotton print
1930
Designed by M. Anufriyeva
Russian Museum, Leningrad
Acquired in 1931.

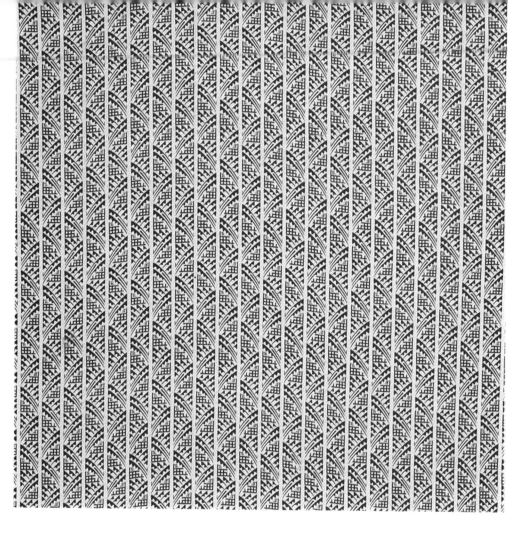

"Rye"
Cotton print
1930
Designed by Bobyshev
Russian Museum, Leningrad
Acquired in 1931.

"Seeding Machines"
Cotton print
1930
Designed by Bobyshev
Russian Museum, Leningrad
Acquired in 1931.

"Tractor"
Cotton print
Late 1920s-early 1930s
Designed by M. Anufriyeva
Russian Museum, Leningrad
Acquired in 1931.

"Young Pioneers' Attributes"
Serge
1929
Designed by Bychkov (?)
Russian Museum, Leningrad
Acquired in 1931.

"International Youth Day"
Cotton print
1929
Designed by M. Nazarevskaya
Russian Museum, Leningrad
Acquired in 1931.

"The Five-Year Plan in Four Years"
Armure
Late 1920s-early 1930s
Designed by Mityaev
Russian Museum, Leningrad
Acquired in 1931.

Coastal Deposition

Q3. Describe what a tombolo is. Name one and say where it is.

....
....
....

Q4. Draw a diagram to explain how a barrier beach forms. Label it to show what happens to the water on the land side of the barrier beach. Name an example.

Q5. As a summary to help you learn, write the heading "Features of Coastal Deposition", then name the <u>four</u> features and give an example of each.

(hint B, S, T, BB)

....
....
....
....
....
....

Life's a beach...

Loads of weird and wonderful landscapes to remember, all formed by the sea moving. And the same old routine — practise the questions, get some wrong, practise the questions, get less wrong, practise the questions, get them all right, have a nice cup of tea to celebrate.

Coasts and People

Stop, look at the title and guess the key word — I'm sorry your time is up, the key word is... people. So expect some more 'affects on people', 'management of problems' type of questions.

Q1. Look at the sketch below showing a coastline that suffers a lot of storms and erosion. Name the different types of sea defences A, B, C and D that are shown.

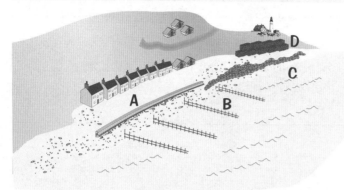

A. ....

B. ....

C. ....

D. ....

Q2. Another kind of defence looks like fences built at the foot of cliffs to protect them from erosion by the waves. What do we call these "fences"?

....

Q3. Complete the table below by detailing the advantages and disadvantages of types of sea defence. You should include how well they work, what they look like and the expense.

Name of the defence	Advantages	Disadvantages

Coasts and People

Q4. Explain why visitors can be a problem in coastal areas.

....

....

....

Q5. Describe <u>three</u> things that can be done to reduce damage to coastal areas by visitors.

1. ....

....

....

2. ....

....

....

3. ....

....

....

Q6. Put the heading "Conflicts of Interest on Coastlines" and write <u>six</u> lines on the different conflicts that can occur on coasts. Think about the opinions of farmers, conservationists, fishermen, boat owners, tourists, residents and authorities such as the National Parks authority.

....

....

....

....

....

....

Coast through the exam — yuk yuk yuk...
Because people live in glaciated and coastal areas (and river areas too) there are often conflicts (you should know what this means by now) and careful management is needed to keep everyone happy.

Glacial Erosion

Movement of ice can have major effects on the landscape. And over the years there's been a lot of ice about. You need to understand how ice causes erosion — glacial erosion.

Q1. Answer these questions:

a) What is the name for the intensely cold periods of the past?

....

b) How many years has it been since the last one?

....

c) What is the name for the "rivers of ice" that flowed over places like Scotland?

....

d) Moving ice erodes the land by two processes – one is abrasion, but what is the other? Explain how each of these processes occurs.

abrasion: ....

.....................: ....

e) Name the type of weathering that caused rock particles to be broken off on the hillsides above the ice. (Hint – F.......T......)

....

f) Describe three ways in which the ice transported its load of rock particles.

....

g) What's it called when the load is dropped?

....

h) Does this usually happen in the mountains or in the lowlands?

....

i) What is the name for the end of the glacier?

....

Q2. Complete these statements:

"How glaciers and rivers are similar"

a) They both start in .... areas.

b) They both flow .... hill.

c) They both have erosion features in .... land areas, and deposition features in .... land areas.

"How glaciers and rivers are different"

d) Glaciers move more ....ly than rivers.

e) Upland river valleys are ..... shaped, whereas upland glaciated valleys are ..... shaped.

Glacial Erosion

Q3. Look at the diagram of an upland area during glaciation.
Name the features A,B,C,D.

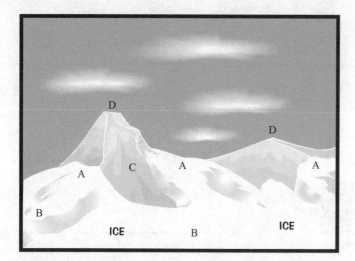

A: ....

B: ....

C: ....

D: ....

Q4. Correct this paragraph about the features above
(circle the right word in each pair):

In the Ice Age, snow and ice collected in hollows in the mountains and started to move in a movement called sensational slip/rotational slip. This movement deepened the hollow by abrasion/attrition and by picking/plucking. The hollow became a feature called a lorry/corrie, and the ice flowed over the lip and downhill as a glacier (feature B/feature C). After the ice melted these hollows often contained a lake called a yarn/tarn. When two corries formed very close together the land between them became eroded and weathered into a gentle/steep ridge called an arete/arrow. The formation of corries, and the biological/freeze thaw weathering which shattered the tops of the mountains above the ice, created jagged peaks called pyramidal/perpendicular peaks.

Q5. Name an example of feature A, feature C and feature D.

A) ....   C) ....

D) ....

Q6. Fill in the gaps to finish these sentences about glacial erosion.

i) The glaciers eroded the valleys like giant bulldozers,
altering the cross profile from a V shape to a .... shape.

ii) Interlocking spurs were removed, leaving steep sides to the valleys known as
.... spurs.

iii) Tributary valleys had smaller glaciers and were not eroded so deeply as the main valley, and so today the tributary valleys are left higher up and are called ....
.... There are often .... where the water flows into the main valley.

Glacial Erosion

Q7. Explain how <u>ribbon lakes</u> are formed.

....

....

....

....

Name an example.

....

Q8. Draw and label a diagram of a roche moutonnee in the box below.
Explain how a <u>roche moutonnee</u> is formed.

....

....

....

....

Q9. As a final check – try to do this from memory:
Write a list called "Ten Features of Glacial Erosion".

Use these first letters to help you:

A ....

C ....

T ....

P.P ....

H.V ....

W ....

T.S ....

R.L ....

G.V ....

R.M ....

Sometimes I think I'm just a walking joke.

ha ha   ha ha   ha ha   ha ha

My nose has worn away — facial erosion...

Glaciation takes thousand of years (to happen, not to learn). But it's not that bad really. The processes aren't too tricky, and then it's just a case of getting your head around a few technical terms. And the best way to do all that — practise these questions till your eyes glaze over.

Glacial Deposition

As well as causing erosion, glaciers can also form landscapes by depositing stuff when they melt...

Q1.   What causes the deposition of a glacier's load?

....

Q2.   Tick the type of material that's deposited by the ice:

☐   rounded particles, nicely sorted into different sizes?

☐   jagged, rough particles, in a jumble of different sizes?

Q3.   Look at the diagram of an area of glacial deposition and name the features A – F.

A: ....

B: ....

C: ....

D: ....

E: ....

F: ....

Q4.   Explain how features A, E and D formed.

....

....

....

....

Q5.   As glaciers melt, meltwater streams flow from the snout. Circle the correct word in each pair:

Meltwater streams coming from melting glaciers carry large loads of rock particles. These are deposited as mouthwash/outwash plains, which are made of organised/disorganised layers of clay mud/sand and gravel. Particles deposited along the channels of meltwater streams, in and under the ice, build up to form ridges called eskers/aretes. Smaller mounds of deposits are called cairns/kames. Deposition areas have shallow depressions or lakes made when blocks of concrete/ice were broken off the melting glacier and became buried by moraine. The surface collapsed when the buried ice melted, forming these features called kettle/rabbit holes.

De position — where de glacier drops de rocks...
The thing about glaciers is that they're <u>not just ice</u> — they've got rocks in 'em. So when they melt, guess what they leave behind... yup, rocks. It's pretty simple, but a lot of people just don't get it.

Section Five — Glaciation

Glaciated Landscapes and People

Look at that title — effects on <u>people</u> rearing its ugly head again.

Q1.   Write a paragraph explaining why glaciated highlands are used for sheep farming.

Hint: A bit on steep gradient; a bit on the weather;
a bit on the poor soils and vegetation; <u>name</u> an example of such an area.

....

....

....

....

....

....

....

Q2.   Many sheep farmers today need to "diversify". What does this mean?

....

....

....

Q3.   Why are glaciated lowlands, like East Anglia, often used for crop farming?

....

....

....

Q4.   Many glaciated highlands have been made into special areas, to protect their beauty.
What are these special areas called? Name two in Britain.

....

....

Glaciated Landscapes and People

Q5. Write a paragraph explaining why glaciated highlands are important for tourism.

....
....
....
....
....
....

Q6. Correct this, by circling the correct word in the pairs:

Glaciated highlands are also used to generate hydro-electric power. Their deep/shallow valleys with their V/U shape and hard/soft rocks are ideal for the building of dams eg in the Scottish Highlands. The light/heavy rainfall soon fills the reservoirs which are also used to supply water to the wetter/drier parts of Britain to the north/south.

Q7. People disagree about land uses in glaciated highlands which leads to "conflicts of interest".
Finish off these sentences to explain some of the different conflicts.

i) Water companies want to build more reservoirs, but farmers don't want this because...

....
....

ii) Tourists visit these areas in their thousands, but farmers get annoyed because...

....
....

iii) Developers build roads, car parks and holiday accommodation, but conservationists argue that...

....
....

iv) Write about another conflict between two types of land use.

....
....
....

Ice down for a full house...

yada yada Physical details... yada yada ... affects on people ... yada yada...
Hmm. Still... practising it now will mean that you'll get it right in the exam. So practise.

World Climate

The weather is a well known English obsession — it's all we ever talk about. Unfortunately it's also pretty popular with geography teachers and Examiners, so get stuck into these...

Q1. World climate zones are classified using which <u>two</u> climate features?

1).. 2)..

Q2. The following figures give a description of Britain's climate:

	Jan	Feb	Mar	Apr	May	Jun	Jul	Aug	Sep	Oct	Nov	Dec
degrees C	5	6	7	9	11	14	15	16	14	11	8	6
mm (total 927)	96	76	51	56	61	54	79	76	76	86	107	110

a) state the maximum temperature ....

b) state the minimum temperature ....

c) state the annual (yearly) temperature range ....

d) is there a dry season? (yes/no) ....

e) Does most rain fall in summer or winter? ....

Q3. What usually happens to temperatures as you go towards the poles (known as the effect of <u>latitude</u>)? Why does this happen?

....

....

Q4. What effect does <u>altitude</u> have on temperatures and rainfall?

....

....

Q5. How does the temperature of inland areas differ from areas on the coast:

a) in summer?

....

b) in winter?

....

c) Why is this?

....

....

Q6. Which areas have a greater temperature range — inland or coastal areas?

....

World Climate

Q7.   What often happens to the amount of rainfall as you go further inland? Why is this?

....

....

Q8.   The <u>factor</u> which is described in questions 5, 6 and 7 is called:

C...

Q9.   Describe how <u>prevailing winds</u> affect the temperature and rainfall of places.

....

....

....

Q10.   The final factor which affects climate is where a place lies (its <u>position</u>)
in relation to the world's wind belts. In which wind belt does Britain lie?

....

Q11.   As a summary of all this, complete the following:
The five factors which affect the climate of a place are

a) L......................, b) A..............................., c) C...........................,

d) P...................W............................ and e) P.............................. .

Q12.   Complete the paragraph by circling the right word in each pair. Use the diagram to help.

Amazonia's climate is hot/cold (about 27 °C) all year round, with a very large/small temperature range of approx 2/20 degrees. Rainfall figures are high/low and rain falls all year round/in one season only. Amazonia lies in the Monsoon/Equatorial climate zone.

Q13.   In what climate zone does Northern Canada lie?

....

Q14.   In Australia and other places in the southern hemisphere, is July in the summer or winter?

....

Warmer, warmer, left a bit, colder, freezing...

Weather's different in different bits of the world. Weather in Australia's brilliant, weather in England isn't — it's that simple. All you need to learn is what sort of weather different areas have and why.

Why It Rains

If the weather is an English obsession — then rain is our specialist subject. After all we get plenty
of it so you should have no excuses for not being an expert — this should be easy...

Q1.   What is precipitation?

....
Name the four types of precipitation.

1)...   2)...

3)...   4)...

Q2.   Fill in these sentences about what causes precipitation.

When air rises and cools, it eventually becomes s....................... with water vapour.

This point is known as the d.......... p..................... and any more cooling causes tiny droplets

of water to c..................... . These tiny droplets form c..................... and eventually the

droplets become big enough to fall as p..................... . This can happen in three ways:

as relief rain, c..................... rain or f................... rain.

Q3.   Draw and label a diagram to explain how relief rain forms.

Q4.   Answer these questions about rain shadows:

a) What is meant by a "rain shadow"?

....

....

b) Is the Lake District an area of rain shadow or relief rain?

....

c) Is Yorkshire an area of rain shadow or relief rain?

....

Section Six — Weather and Climate

Why It Rains

Q5. What is the name of the type of rainfall that forms due to the Sun's heat in hot countries (or even in Britain in summer)?

....

Circle the right words from each pair in this paragraph:

The Sun heats the ground and the air above it becomes cool/warm and it rises/falls by confusion/convection. As it rises/falls, it warms/cools until the water vapour evaporates/condenses, forming thick/thin clouds. Often very large clouds called stratus/cumulonimbus form, which bring drizzle/heavy rain and meteorites/thunder and lightning.

Q6. Answer these questions about frontal rain:

a) What is a "front"?

....

....

b) What kind of rain falls at a cold front?

....

....

c) What kind of rain falls at a warm front?

....

....

d) Do these fronts occur in weather systems called lows (depressions) or highs (anticyclones)?

....

e) Name a country that receives a lot of frontal rainfall.

....

Why does it always rain on me — It's a Travisty...

There's more to rain than just getting you wet and spoiling your picnic. There's different types of rain and different ways in which it's caused. So next time it's pouring down and everyone's whinging, you can marvel at the mysteries of geography.

Synoptic Charts

Weathermen record loads of information and study maps and charts in their vain attempt to predict the weather. But they do their best, and they do have a fine array of charts...

Q1.   Answer these questions:

a) Name the four main types of data that are measured by weather stations.

1)...   2)..

3)...   4)..

b) What is the common name for synoptic charts?

....

c) What is meant by atmospheric or air pressure?

....

d) On maps, what are the lines called that join places of equal air pressure?

....

e) Do these lines show air pressure in metres or millibars?

....

Q2.   Draw the correct weather symbols for the following:

rain	snow showers	mist	drizzle	thunderstorm

Q3.   Look at the diagram below. State five facts about the weather that this weather station is having.

1)...   4)...

2)...   5)...

3)...

<u>Synoptic Charts</u>

Q4.   Look at the diagrams and answer the questions underneath.

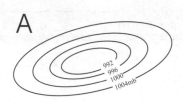

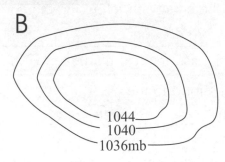

What are the two names for the weather system in diagram A? ....

and the two names for B? ....

Q5.   Give two reasons why satellite images are useful to weathermen.

....

....

Q6.   What colour do dense clouds appear on a satellite image?

....

Q7.   What colour does the sea appear
on a satellite image?

....

<u>One eyed weather maps — cycloptic charts...</u>

It's pretty complicated all this recording and predicting the weather — no wonder Michael Fish
gets it wrong once in a while. But just because he makes mistakes, doesn't mean you can.
If you want good marks there's no easy solution, just keep practising.

Lows and Highs

You have to cope with pressure and learn about it for your exams. These questions should help with the learning part. As for coping — consult a yoga expert (if you find tying your legs in knots relaxing)...

Q1. Complete the paragraph, choosing the correct words from this list.
Use each word only once.

polar; north east; tropical maritime; west; south; fronts; north; low; polar front; less dense.

Depressions form to the .... of Britain, where warm moist ....
air from the .... meets cold .... air from the ...., along a zone
called the .... The warmer .... air rises above
the colder air, creating .... pressure at the ground. The boundaries between the warm and
cold air are called ...., and the whole system travels .... wards across Britain,
bringing a characteristic set of weather conditions.

Q2. Look at this weather map of a depression. Label on it:

the centre of the low;
the warm front;
the cold front;
the cold polar air;
the warm tropical air.

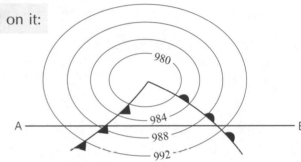

Q3. Look at the cross-section across the depression, along X–Y. People at the weather station can observe what happens as the depression moves over them.

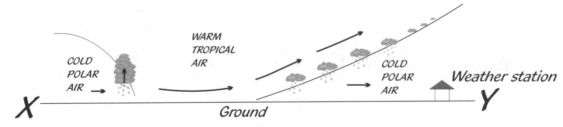

Circle the twelve pairs in the description of what they observe:

First the temperature is warm/cold and high above are some wispy cirrus/cumulonimbus clouds. Gradually it starts to drizzle and rain/get more sunny. Then the cold/warm air known as the warm sector passes over so that temperatures rise/fall and the rain starts/stops. After a few hours the cold/warm front has moved eastwards, pushing up the warm air ahead of/behind it to produce larger clouds and heavy/light rain. Then it becomes warm/cold and windy in the polar/tropical air as the winds change direction (they "veer"/"peer") from southwesterly to northwesterly.

Q4. What is an occluded front (occlusion)?

....

....

Section Six — Weather and Climate

Lows and Highs

Q5. For each of these statements about highs (anticyclones) tick the True or False box:

True False
a) ☐ ☐ They bring wet weather.
b) ☐ ☐ They bring windy weather.
c) ☐ ☐ They bring clear skies.
d) ☐ ☐ In winter, temperatures rise at night because skies are so cloudy.
e) ☐ ☐ By day the weather is often bright and sunny.
f) ☐ ☐ In summer, they often bring Britain a heat wave (over 25 °C).

Q6. Explain why frost often forms during an anticyclone on winter nights.

....
....
....
....

Q7. Answer these questions about temperature inversion:

What is meant by "temperature inversion"?

....
....

What weather feature is often caused by this and what is this feature also known as?
(A......... G.........)

....
....

Q8. Complete the table to detail the differences between a depression and an anticyclone:

Feature	Depression	Anticyclone
Air Pressure		
Winds		
Cloudiness		
Summer Temperatures		
Winter Temperatures		
Rain		

Weather Hazards — Fog

Severe weather conditions can be a serious hazard causing major damage and even death. You need to know about these hazards and how people cope with them.

Q1.   Circle the right words out of each pair to complete this definition of fog:

Fog is made of oxygen/droplets of water suspended in the lower/upper layers of the atmosphere, resulting from evaporation/condensation of water vapour/carbon dioxide around nuclei of dust or smoke/food particles.

Q2.   Explain how advection fog forms and draw a diagram of it.

Name an area which has this type of fog.

....

....

....

....

....

....

....

....

Q3.   Look at the diagram:

WARM AIR

warm front

COLD AIR

Fog

Ground

a) Why does fog form in this part of a depression?

....

....

....

b) Name this type of fog.

....

Section Six — Weather and Climate

Weather Hazards — Fog

Q4. Look at the diagram then finish the explanations for this type of fog.

a) It is night and the sky is c................... .

b) The ground cools by r................... .

c) This chills the air next to it

to the d.......... p................ .

d) The water vapour c................... to form droplets.

e) A light w................... lifts the droplets into the air, forming fog.

f) This kind of fog is called r................... f....... .

g) This kind of fog forms in spring, ... and ...., but not usually in ....

Q5. Explain how steam fog forms. Name an area where it is common.

....

....

....

....

Q6. Answer these questions about smog:

a) How does smog differ from fog?

....

....

b) Does smog form in urban or rural areas?

....

c) What are condensation nuclei and how do they help the formation of smog?

....

....

d) Name an example of a place that has a lot of smog.

....

Q7. Describe two hazards that people may face due to fog or smog.

....

....

Gor blimey — it's a real pea souper, Guv...

With any weather hazard you need to learn the same stuff — what causes it, how it affects people and how they cope. It's the same old routine with all this physical geography — get used to it.

Section Six — Weather and Climate

Weather Hazards — Hurricanes

Fog may not have sounded like a major problem but hurricanes certainly are...

Q1.   Is a hurricane an area of low or high pressure?

....

Q2.   Give one other name for hurricanes and state in which part of the world this name is used.

....

Q3.   Tick the correct box to show the part of the world where hurricanes start:

a) ☐   In the middle latitudes, around 50º N.

b) ☐   On either side of the Equator, between 8º and 15º N and S.

c) ☐   Near the poles.

Q4.   At what time of year do hurricanes occur?   ....

Q5.   Correct this paragraph, by circling the correct words out of the twelve pairs:

Hurricanes form over cold/warm oceans where the temperature is over 26 ºC/100 ºC.
The Sun's energy evaporates/condenses the sea water and causes the warmed, moist air
to fall/rise rapidly, forming an intense spiral of air called a vortex/complex. The rising
air cools until the water vapour evaporates/condenses, forming small/huge clouds and rain.
The condensation releases vast amounts of heat which keeps providing the energy to fuel
the hurricane. It becomes a moving, rotating storm with very light/very strong winds of
around 1600/160 km per hour. It travels westwards and towards the poles/Equator.
A hurricane eventually dies out either because it has reached warmer/colder areas or
because it moved over land/over sea where it loses its energy source.

Q6.   Answer these questions:

a) What is the central part of a hurricane called?   ....

b) How many km across is this area?   ....

c) What kind of weather occurs here?   ....

d) Is the air rising or falling here?   ....

Q7.   On average, how many hurricanes occur over the world per year?

....

Q8.   On average, how many people die each year in hurricanes?

....

Q9.   From this list write down the five places which have hurricanes:

Japan; Australia; Sweden; the Caribbean; China; Peru; Bangladesh; Alaska.

....

Local Weather

**All sorts of different factors can affect the weather. Some of the factors are
very local — so take a walk 'on the sunny side of the street'...**

Q1. Define the word "microclimate".

....

....

Q2. Look at this map of temperatures over a British city and answer the questions below:

a) Describe what you observe about the pattern of temperatures.

....

....

b) What is this effect called?

....

c) Give three reasons for this effect.

....

....

....

d) Is this effect more noticeable by day or night? Give two reasons why.

....

....

e) Give one reason why this effect is greater in many
U.S. cities (such as New York) than in British cities.

....

....

Q3. Why do urban areas receive less sunshine than rural areas?

....

....

Q4. Compared to nearby rural areas, do cities have more or less: rain; cloud; fog? Why?

....

....

Section Six — Weather and Climate

Local Weather

Q5. Describe two ways in which buildings in cities affect windspeeds.

....

....

Q6. Look at the diagram of part of Amazonia and answer the questions below.

a) Which area will be less windy and why — A or B?

....

b) Which area will be hotter by day and why — A or B?

....

c) Which area will be warmer by night and why — A or B?

....

d) Which area will be drier – A or B? Give two reasons why.

....

....

e) Which area will absorb more of the Sun's heat and why — A or B?

....

Q7. Draw a labelled diagram to explain how aspect affects local climate.

Local Weather

Q8. Answer these questions on water areas and microclimate:

a) Give two reasons why these areas have more cloud, rain and fog.

....

....

b) Give one reason why they are more windy than land areas.

....

....

c) In summer, are water areas cooler or warmer by day than land areas?

....

d) In winter, are water areas cooler or warmer by day than land areas?

....

e) Explain why c) and d) occur.

....

....

Q9. Complete this sentence:

The factors which affect microclimate are u..................... and

r..................... areas; the c................... of the surface; a...................;

w............... or l............... areas; and v........................ .

Q10. Name the weather instruments which measure:

a) temperature   ....

b) rainfall   ....

c) wind direction   ....

Q11. What do the following measure?

a) barometer   ....

b) anemometer   ....

Ecosystems

Ecosystems — what could be more fun than these little beauties. And in this section you also get lots of questions about...wait for it...soil. Oh, joy of joys.

Q1. Complete this definition of an ecosystem:

"An ecosystem is a community of l........................... t...........................

which live together in a certain e...........................".

Q2. The world is divided into large ecosystem units. What is the name for these units?

....

Q3. Name the ecosystem unit that occurs:

a) around the Equator;

....

b) in Britain;

....

c) in the far north of Canada.

....

Q4. Name the <u>four</u> main factors that affect the distribution of world vegetation types.

1. ....

2. ....

3. ....

4. ....

There's nothing funny about ecosystems...

If you get away with not answering a question on ecosystems in your Exam, then I'm a flying hippo. If you've got any sense, you'll learn this stuff real well. It's the only way.

Deserts and Tundra

Both these environments are pretty inhospitable, and so I've lumped them together.
Do the questions, and as you do them, remember how much fun you're having.

Q1.   Name two of the world's deserts.

1. ....   2. ....

Q2.   What two features of desert rainfall make it difficult for plants to grow?

1. ....

2. ....

Q3.   Describe three ways in which desert plants are adapted to the desert climate.

1. ....

2. ....

3. ....

Q4.   Complete the paragraph about tundra, by circling the correct words from each pair.

The Tundra biome is near the Equator/near the poles, eg North Canada/Brazil. The climate

makes plant life difficult because of the low/high temperatures, the high/low precipitation

and the windy/calm conditions. The ground is soft/frozen for much of

the year — this is known as thermafrost/permafrost. Plants therefore have to have

short/long roots and all plants are tall/small, usually below 30 cm/above 3m tall.

Q5.   Name four different types of plants which grow in the Tundra.

1. ....   3. ....

2. ....   4. ....

I hate being tundra...

Amazing, some things will grow <u>anywhere</u>. Dandelions, for example. Well no, *they* won't grow in
the desert, but there *are* things that will — and stuff grows in the frozen wastes of the Arctic, too.
What you need to <u>learn</u> is how all of these plants are <u>adapted</u> to their environment, whatever it is.

Tropical Rainforests

Tropical rainforests seem to be in the news quite a lot these days.
And it's bad news, so stop blowing your nose unless it's on recycled paper...

Q1.   This question is all about tropical rainforests — hurrah.

a) What type of climate is usually found in these areas?

....

b) Name one area where this type of ecosystem is found.

....

c) Describe the temperature and rainfall of this area.

....

....

d) Does this area have very different seasons or no definite seasons?

....

e) How does that affect the way in which plants grow?

....

f) What are the dominant (main) plants — grasses or trees?

....

g) Which of the following is NOT a rainforest plant — mahogany; starfish; teak?

....

h) Describe the usual shape of rainforest leaves. Why are they like this?

....

i) Are there few species found in these areas or many different ones?

....

Tropical Rainforests

Q2. Look at the diagram and answer the questions below.

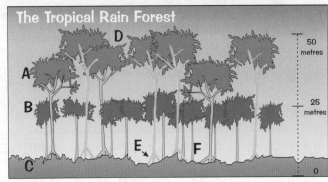

a) Name layers A, B and C.

Layer A: ....

Layer B: ....

Layer C: ....

b) What are trees like D called? How tall can they be?

....

c) What shape are the tree crowns (tops)? Why?

....

....

d) Name the features at E. What are they for?

....

....

e) What are light levels like at F?

....

f) How does this affect layer C?

....

....

g) Name two other types of plant that are in layer B.

.... and ....

I hate being a tree...

There's quite a lot they can ask you about tropical rainforests. If you got any of these answers wrong, you need to get your revising boots on and wade in (sorry).

Section Seven — Ecosystems and Soils

Tropical Grassland

Another page — another biome for you to answer questions about.
You might not think it's fun, but on Exam day you'll certainly be glad you did it.

Q1. Complete this paragraph, circling the correct words from each of the ten pairs.

Tropical grassland is found to the west and east/north and south of tropical rainforest.
Two areas where this biome occurs are Italy and Greece/Kenya and Ethiopia. The
climate here has definite wet and dry seasons/is the same all year round and it is hot.
The dominant plants are grasses/trees which are tough and spiky/soft and delicate, and
short/tall. They can be about 3m/3mm tall and drought-resistant. An example is
pampas/pompous grass. The grasses form clumps with little/a lot of bare soil in
between, and they grow well/die down in the dry season.

Q2. Describe three ways in which scattered trees in tropical
grasslands are adapted to cope with the dry season.

1. ....

2. ....

3. ....

Name one tree from this biome.

....

Q3. Tropical grassland is called "plagioclimax vegetation". What does this mean?

....

....

You should try being a blade of grass mate...

Tropical grasslands are great. Remember that, as you're slaving away over your revision books,
thinking exactly the opposite. If I can't convince you it's interesting, at least admit there's every
chance it'll be in the Exam, and learn it anyway.

Section Seven — Ecosystems and Soils

Temperate Grassland and Mediterranean

The Med — ahhh, fond memories of holidays past, and holidays future. Sigh...
Anyway, back to reality — you need to know all the usual stuff about two more biomes.

Q1. Read these sentences which are supposed to describe
temperate grasslands and circle "TRUE" or "FALSE" for each.

a) These areas are cooler lands which are no use for farming.   TRUE   FALSE

b) These areas are cooler lands which are important for cereal
and animal farming.   TRUE   FALSE

c) The natural vegetation of these areas is a dense cover of
many grasses, with a few trees in wetter areas.   TRUE   FALSE

d) This biome has dense woodland with undergrowth of astroturf.   TRUE   FALSE

e) Two areas of temperate grassland are Britain and Greenland.   TRUE   FALSE

f) Two areas of temperate grassland are the Prairies of the USA
and the Steppes of Asia.   TRUE   FALSE

Q2. Complete this paragraph about Mediterranean regions
by circling the correct word from each of the ten pairs.

This biome is found in countries like Italy and Greece/Norway and Sweden around

30 – 40 N and S/50 – 60 N and S. These areas have cold and wet/hot and dry summers.

Centuries of crop farming and grazing/pizza production have removed the original

vegetation which was grassland/evergreen forest and which could tolerate the summer's

drought/saturated soils. Today, plants like thorny shrubs/ferns grow as well as aromatic

plants like thyme/cacti and rosemary. They have very small/very large waxy leaves to

reduce/increase water loss.

Turf's up dude...
Temperate grasslands and Mediterranean regions — remember what they're like, and where they are.
Job's a good'un.

Temperate Deciduous Forest

Another biome — which means chuckles aplenty. But to the examiner it's just another thing to catch you out on. Learn the ways of the temperate deciduous forest.

Q1.   Name **two** areas where temperate deciduous forests are found.

1. ....

2. ....

Q2.   What does "deciduous" mean?

....

....

Q3.   Describe each of these three layers and name two species that form part of each one:

a) The tree layer

....

....

b) The shrub layer

....

....

c) Ground cover

....

....

Can't see the temperate deciduous forest for the trees...

OK — I admit this isn't as much fun as tucking into those cream-covered banana cakes you get in the baker's, but it's not so bad really. And you can at least see some temperate deciduous forest without having to travel thousands of miles. (Ooooh... a clue, how lovely.)

Coniferous Forest

Conifers — the ones with those cool-looking cones. You can spray them silver and use them as Christmas decorations. If you like that sort of thing.

Q1. Which one of these three words best describes the climate of the coniferous forest biome?

MILD   HARSH   COOL

Q2. Name two areas where this biome is found.

.... and ....

Q3. Complete this table describing coniferous trees.

Feature	Description	Reason
Tree	Evergreen	
Shape		
Branches	Flexible	
Roots		
Leaves	Needles	
Cones		

Q4. Name two plant species which grow in coniferous forests.

....

....

Q5. Explain why there is little undergrowth in a coniferous forest.

....

....

Man cannot live on tree gags alone...

Coniferous forests — not to be confused with carnivorous forests, full of those vicious man-eating trees. But anyway, back in the real world... they can be strange, spooky environments, these coniferous forests, and it's all to do with things on this page. And it gets weirder on page 65.

Soil

And now, the bit we've all been waiting for... loads of questions about soil.
Yep... page after page full of questions about dirt. Enjoy.

Q1.   Look at the pie chart and answer the questions.

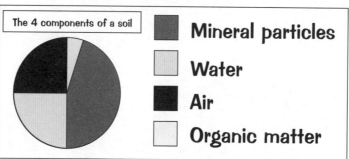

The 4 components of a soil

■ Mineral particles
□ Water
■ Air
□ Organic matter

a) What is the biggest component of the soil?

....

b) Does this make up about 30% or 45% of the soil?

....

c) What percentage of the soil is water?

....

d) What percentage of the soil is air?

....

e) Give four examples of things that make up the organic matter.

1. ....   3. ....

2. ....   4. ....

Q2.   Which **two** colours are very common in tropical soils?

.... and ....

Q3.   Which mineral is very common in tropical soils?

....

Soil ....**_it's more exciting than you'd think_**
Indeed.

Section Seven — Ecosystems and Soils

Soil Processes

And it's not just questions about the make up of soil I've included.
No Siree — you've got questions about what happens in soil too...

Q1.   Complete these two paragraphs by circling the correct word from each pair.

a) Leaching is caused by rainfall/sunlight moving down through the soil. It dissolves any

insoluble/soluble minerals and washes them down to lower layers. A lot of leaching causes

soils to become less/more fertile.

b) Podsolisation is a process that occurs under deciduous/coniferous trees, where the rain is

made more/less acidic by the needles. The rain dissolves the minerals and washes them

down, leaving the upper soil paler/darker in colour. The soil becomes

red-brown/pale ash-grey. The lower soil receives these minerals and becomes paler/darker,

with a red-brown/pale ash-grey colour. These soils (called podsols) are infertile/fertile.

Q2.   Are the following statements about gleying true or false? Circle the right answers.

a) Gleying occurs under waterlogged conditions.   TRUE   FALSE

b) Gley soils usually form in valley bottoms.   TRUE   FALSE

Q3.   Explain why gley soils have a blue-grey colour.

....

....

Q4.   Answer these questions about desert soils.

a) Why does water move upwards through desert soils?

....

b) What happens on or near the surface as a result?

....

....*maybe...*

If you got all the answers right, you can move on to the next section. If not, back to the books.

More About Soil

As well as being important for your Exam, this stuff is great for talking about at parties.

Q1.   Complete the following sentences about acidity.

a)   Acidity is measured on a log scale of 1 to ....

b)   If a soil is tested and measures 5.0, it is ....

c)   If it measures 8.0, it is ....

Q2.   Name the mineral which gives many soils a red colour.

....

Q3.   Define soil texture and name a type of soil texture.

....

....

Q4.   "The ways in which the particles are stuck together and arranged" is the definition of which soil characteristic?

....

Q5.   Look at the incorrect soil profile and answer the questions that follow.

a)   Re-draw the diagram, putting the layers in the correct order.

b)   Name this type of soil.

....

c)   Name the biome and a country in which it occurs.

Biome: ....   Country: ....

Processes in Ecosystems

A bit more about ecosystems — this time questions about processes going on all the time.

Q1. A food chain is an example of the links in an ecosystem. Complete this simple food chain.

Grass ⟶ [..................................] ⟶ Fox

Q2. Correct this paragraph by circling the right words from each pair.

Green plants are very important in ecosystems as they are the

primary consumers/primary producers. This means that they use energy from the Sun/Moon

to make food by a process called photography/photosynthesis. They also use water and

nutrients from the soil/supermarket. Plants are then eaten by herbivores, e.g. lion/sheep,

while other animals known as carnivals/carnivores eat the herbivores.

Q3. Choose the correct word from each pair. Then complete the photosynthesis equation.

Oxygen / Carbon dioxide + Soil / Water + Sunlight ⟶ Starch / Sugar + ... + ...

Q4. The carbon cycle — by what process does carbon enter the air from:

a) industrial areas? ....

b) human damage to tropical rainforests? ....

Q5. Draw and label a simple diagram to show the nitrogen cycle.

Q6. Explain why bacteria are useful when plants and animals die.

....

Food chains — it's a dog eat dog food world out there...
Phew, lots there — but about as important as it comes. Have a cup of tea if you got them all.

Ecosystems and the Human Effects

After all those pages about ecosystems, it's time for a few questions about how people affect the areas in which they live, and the consequences of their actions.

Q1.   Give one reason for each of the following:

a) The felling (by people) of the temperate deciduous forest of Britain.

....

b) The destruction of the natural vegetation in the temperate grasslands of North America.

....

Q2.   If left undisturbed, natural vegetation will develop through time to become the "climatic climax vegetation". Write a definition of this.

....

....

Q3.   What is a "plagioclimax community" of vegetation?

....

....

Q4.   Which of these is <u>not</u> a region of plagioclimax vegetation? Circle the correct answer.

Mediterranean   Tundra   tropical grassland

Q5.   Finish the labels on this diagram of human effects.

a) 1945-85: Half of Nepal's trees were felled (this is d ....) to create farmland for the rapidly ....
    ....

b) Too much cultivation, grazing on s .... slopes of the H ....

c) All this caused a huge increase in r .... and s .... e ....

d) Large amounts of sediment were carried down and deposited, raising the bed of the River ....

River Ganges   SEA

e) All of this increased the risk of f .... in B ....

Human effects on ecosystems — basically we muck it all up...

It's in the news all the time — the effect people are having on various ecosystems — and so it's likely to be a favoured topic among examiners. Don't skimp on the revision of this topic.

Deforestation and Conservation

Another hot topic with far reaching effects. Get stuck in.

Q1.   What is the name for the natural vegetation in the Amazonian part of Brazil?

....

Q2.   Describe why this vegetation is being destroyed. Include the following ideas in your answer.

logging   population increase   cattle ranching   mining   HEP developments

....

....

....

....

Q3.   Answer these questions about Western Siberia.

a)   What industry led to the deforestation of so many coniferous trees in Western Siberia?

....

b)   What other environmental problem has this industry caused?

....

c)   Will the forest ecosystem recover easily or not in this area? Give reasons.

....

....

....

Tree felled to make book to warn about felling trees — oops...

It's amazing the effect people can have on their environment, and that's why it's vitally important that you should know as much as possible about this stuff. There's also the issue of a fast-approaching exam, which is, of course, another reason why you should know it.

The Arguments for Conserving Forests

These two pages are about the arguments for conserving forests and those
in favour of deforestation. You have to know both sets of arguments.

Q1. Explain why long-term farming in tropical rainforests is never a success.

....

....

Q2. How could the forest benefit human health?

....

....

Q3. Why do native tribes want to conserve the tropical rainforest?

....

....

Q4. Answer the following questions on the ways deforestation affects the climate.

a) Why does keeping the forest in place help to combat global warming?

....

....

b) How is the rate of evapotranspiration altered by deforestation
and what effect will this have?

....

....

....

The Arguments for Deforestation

Q1. Use either the letter L or the letter M to complete these arguments in favour of deforestation.

> 1. ...... EDCs like Thailand and Brazil are destroying their tropical rainforest and selling timber because they are poorer than ...... EDCs.

> 2. ...... EDCs are in debt to ...... EDCs, and so have to sell whatever resources they have, eg timber and iron ore from Amazonia.

> 3. As long as ...... EDCs like the USA and Japan keep buying these products, there is nothing to encourage ...... EDCs to stop the deforestation.

Q2. Describe **two** things that MEDCs could do to help LEDCs reduce deforestation.

1. ....

2. ....

Q3. Malaysia has a "sustainable" (i.e. environmentally friendly, non-damaging for the future) timber industry. Explain two restrictions placed on timber companies in Malaysia.

1. ....

....

2. ....

....

I'm stumped...

Well there you go — it's a complicated debate. Whichever side you actually believe in, you have to know the arguments on the <u>other side</u> as well to get top marks in the Exam. It's not enough to just rant on about what <u>you</u> believe, you have to make a <u>reasoned argument</u>.

Section Eight — Maps

Blimey. Maps? In full colour? Skip to the questions on page 80.

Key

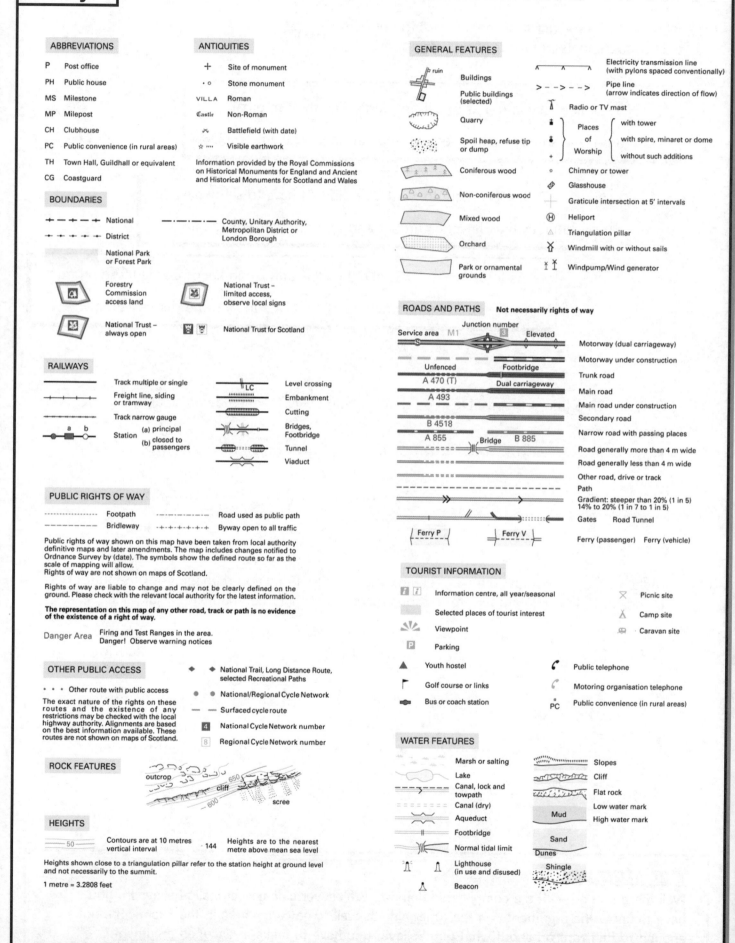

ABBREVIATIONS

P   Post office
PH   Public house
MS   Milestone
MP   Milepost
CH   Clubhouse
PC   Public convenience (in rural areas)
TH   Town Hall, Guildhall or equivalent
CG   Coastguard

BOUNDARIES

+ — + — +   National

+ — • + — • —   District

County, Unitary Authority, Metropolitan District or London Borough

National Park or Forest Park

Forestry Commission access land

National Trust – always open

National Trust – limited access, observe local signs

National Trust for Scotland

RAILWAYS

Track multiple or single

Freight line, siding or tramway

Track narrow gauge

Station   (a) principal   (b) closed to passengers

Level crossing

Embankment

Cutting

Bridges, Footbridge

Tunnel

Viaduct

PUBLIC RIGHTS OF WAY

··············   Footpath

— — — — —   Bridleway

— • — • — •   Road used as public path

+ + + + + +   Byway open to all traffic

Public rights of way shown on this map have been taken from local authority definitive maps and later amendments. The map includes changes notified to Ordnance Survey by (date). The symbols show the defined route so far as the scale of mapping will allow.
Rights of way are not shown on maps of Scotland.

Rights of way are liable to change and may not be clearly defined on the ground. Please check with the relevant local authority for the latest information.

The representation on this map of any other road, track or path is no evidence of the existence of a right of way.

Danger Area   Firing and Test Ranges in the area. Danger! Observe warning notices

OTHER PUBLIC ACCESS

◆ • • ◆   National Trail, Long Distance Route, selected Recreational Paths

• • •   Other route with public access

The exact nature of the rights on these routes and the existence of any restrictions may be checked with the local highway authority. Alignments are based on the best information available. These routes are not shown on maps of Scotland.

●   ●   National/Regional Cycle Network

—   —   Surfaced cycle route

4   National Cycle Network number

8   Regional Cycle Network number

ROCK FEATURES

outcrop   cliff   650   600   scree

HEIGHTS

— 50 —   Contours are at 10 metres vertical interval

144   Heights are to the nearest metre above mean sea level

Heights shown close to a triangulation pillar refer to the station height at ground level and not necessarily to the summit.

1 metre = 3.2808 feet

ANTIQUITIES

+   Site of monument
• ○   Stone monument
VILLA   Roman
Castle   Non-Roman
⚔   Battlefield (with date)
☆ ····   Visible earthwork

Information provided by the Royal Commissions on Historical Monuments for England and Ancient and Historical Monuments for Scotland and Wales

GENERAL FEATURES

ruin   Buildings

Public buildings (selected)

Quarry

Spoil heap, refuse tip or dump

Coniferous wood

Non-coniferous wood

Mixed wood

Orchard

Park or ornamental grounds

Electricity transmission line (with pylons spaced conventionally)

> – –> – –>   Pipe line (arrow indicates direction of flow)

Radio or TV mast

Places of Worship   { with tower
with spire, minaret or dome
without such additions }

○   Chimney or tower
⌀   Glasshouse
+   Graticule intersection at 5' intervals
Ⓗ   Heliport
△   Triangulation pillar
ⵜ   Windmill with or without sails
ⵜ   Windpump/Wind generator

ROADS AND PATHS   Not necessarily rights of way

Service area   M1   Junction number   3   Elevated

Motorway (dual carriageway)

Motorway under construction

Unfenced   Footbridge   Trunk road

A 470 (T)   Dual carriageway   Main road

A 493   Main road under construction

B 4518   Secondary road

A 855   Bridge   B 885   Narrow road with passing places

Road generally more than 4 m wide

Road generally less than 4 m wide

Other road, drive or track

Path

Gradient: steeper than 20% (1 in 5) 14% to 20% (1 in 7 to 1 in 5)

Gates   Road Tunnel

Ferry P   Ferry V   Ferry (passenger)   Ferry (vehicle)

TOURIST INFORMATION

i i   Information centre, all year/seasonal

Selected places of tourist interest

Viewpoint

P   Parking

▲   Youth hostel

⚑   Golf course or links

Bus or coach station

✕   Picnic site
⋀   Camp site
Caravan site

☎   Public telephone

☎   Motoring organisation telephone

PC   Public convenience (in rural areas)

WATER FEATURES

Marsh or salting
Lake
Canal, lock and towpath
Canal (dry)
Aqueduct
Footbridge
Normal tidal limit
Lighthouse (in use and disused)
Beacon

Slopes
Cliff
Flat rock
Low water mark
Mud   High water mark
Sand
Dunes
Shingle

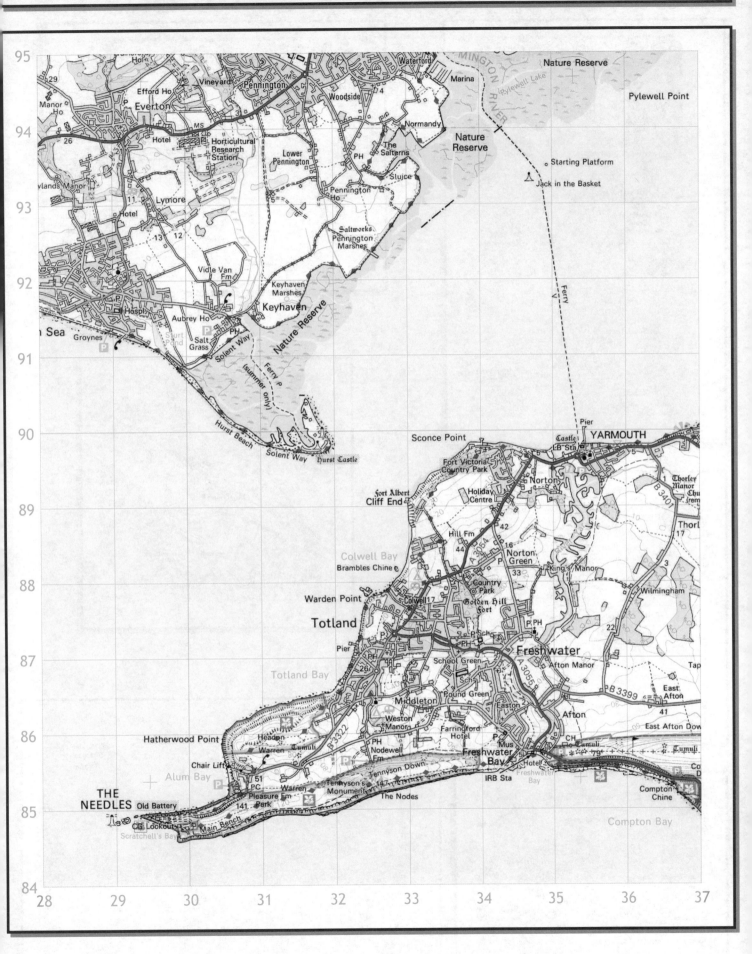

One Kilometre   One Mile

Section Eight — Maps

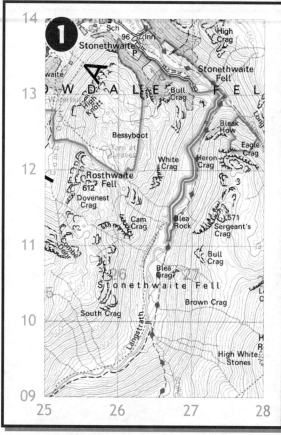

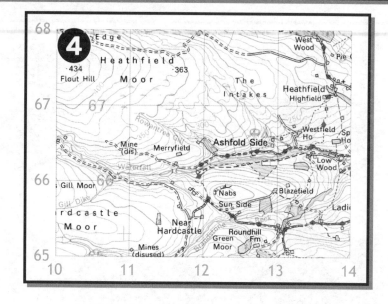

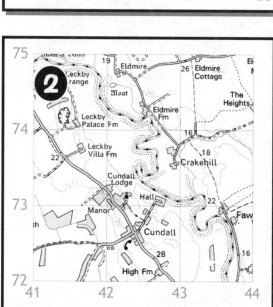

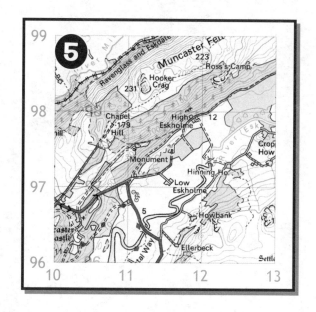

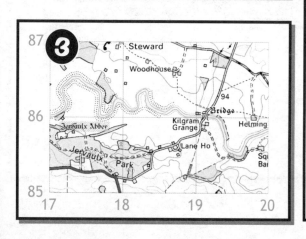

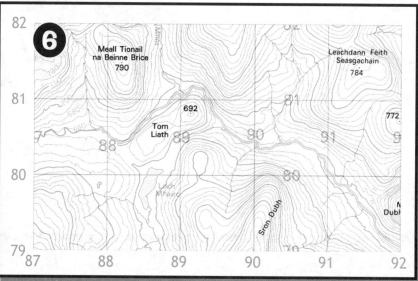

One Kilometre   One Mile

Section Eight — Maps

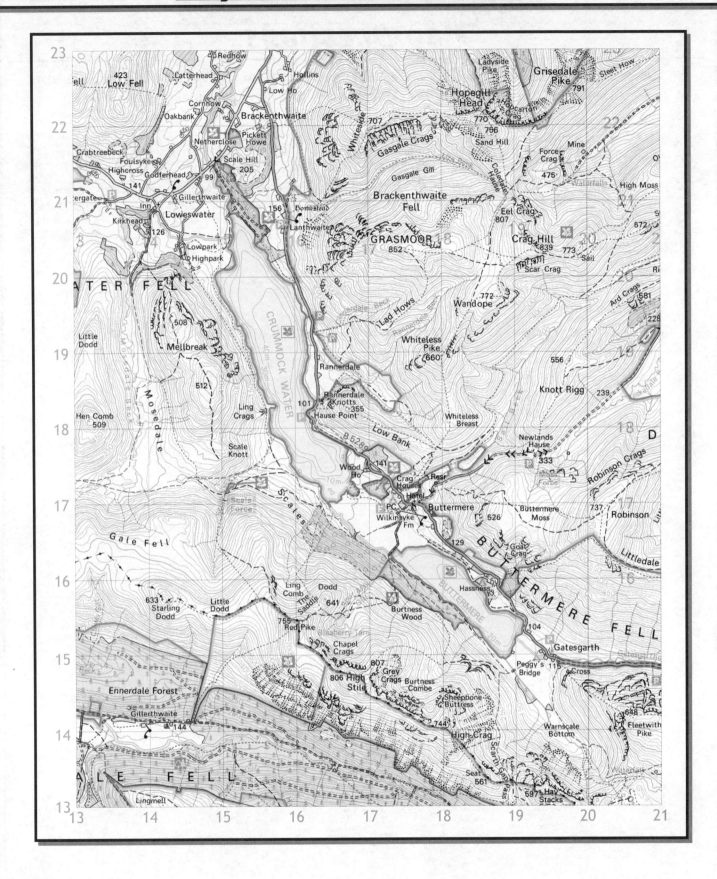

One Kilometre   One Mile

Section Eight — Maps

Map Questions

Don't all those maps look beautiful... but I'm afraid they're not just there to brighten your day.
They're so you can answer these questions — you don't get nothing for nothing...

Q1. Look at the map of the part of Isle of Wight
on p73 and answer these questions:

a) Identify the large spit on the map by giving the grid square containing its south east corner.

....

b) Name the building on it: ....

c) What is the feature between grid 310849 and 320850? ....

d) On the sketch copy of the map below, draw in the coastline of the Isle of Wight:

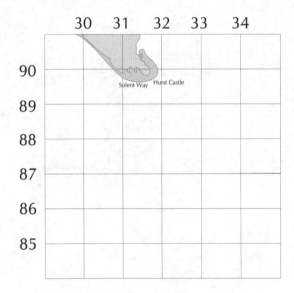

Q2. Look at the river maps on p74
and answer these questions:

a) For each map say whether it shows the upper or lower stage of the river:

    Map 1 ....
    Map 2 ....
    Map 3 ....
    Map 4 ....
    Map 5 ....
    Map 6 ....

b) In map 4 give the six-figure grid reference of the waterfall. ....

c) In map 2 identify the feature at 425735. ....

d) In map 6 is the river running from left to right or right to left? ....

Map Questions

Q3.   Look at the map of Crummock Water on p75 and answer the following questions:

a) The river changes direction at 151211. What is this feature called?

....

b) Look at the feature marked, 'Scale Force' at 151171. What do you think this feature is?

....

c) Complete the following sentences about contour lines:
Contour lines join points of equal h .... They are used on the maps
to show how s .... the ground is. The c .... the contour
lines are, the s .... the ground is.

d) Use the map of Crummock Water and its contour lines to draw a cross-section of the
landscape and lake between the Grasmoor peak in 1720 and the Mellbreak peak in 1419.

e) What formed the valley containing Crummock Water and Buttermere?

....

f) What glacial feature contains Bleabury Tarn (1615)?

....

g) How was it formed?

....
....
....

ꟼ∀W — I think it goes the other way up...

It's important that you get used to using maps and recognising different features on them.
Practice makes perfect, especially to stop silly little mistakes like getting your coordinates the
wrong way round. So keep doing these questions until you can do them in your sleep.

Section Eight — Maps

Section Nine — Answers

Pages 1 – 12

Page 1

Q1 a) plates b) convection currents in the mantle c) a few mm/yr
d) plate boundaries/margins.

Q2 a) destructive margin – moving together, eg The Nazca Plate in
South America.
b) conservative margin – moving sideways, eg the San Andreas
Fault in California.
c) constructive margin – the plates move apart; new material rises
up/extruded eg in the Mid Atlantic.

Q3 Fold Mountains.

Pages 2, 3

Q1 a) extinct b) eg Arthur's Seat, Edinburgh c) dormant
d) eg Santorini, Greece e) active f) eg Mt Etna, Sicily g) 600
h) "Ring of Fire" i) constructive and destructive

Q2 Labels: 1. Volcanic bombs 2. Secondary cone 3. Ash and lava
4. Vent 5. Volcanic ash 6. Gas 7. Crater 8. Lava
9. Magma, magma chamber 10. eg Mt Etna, Sicily

Q3 *Shield volcano* – lava is runny, basic, flows quickly and takes
longer to harden, the volcano is therefore a large, wide, flat
mountain eg Mauna Loa, in Hawaii. *Dome volcano* – lava is
thicker, acid, flows slowly and hardens quickly. The volcano is
therefore a steepsided, dome shape eg Mt St Helens, USA.

Page 4

Q1 missing words are: seismic; focus; epicentre; seismometer
(seismograph is ok); magnitude; Richter; ten.

Q2 Japan, California, Mexico.

Q3 a) people asleep, unaware of danger – falling buildings.
b) possible ideas – poor warnings, people not informed of danger
(poor communications, disease afterwards due to dirty water).
c) destruction of expensive shops, buildings, cars…
d) very low population density in Alaska, far fewer buildings.

Pages 5, 6

Q1 a) volcanic rocks weather to produce fertile soil
b) wonderful climate, cheap land, because settled there.

Q2 a) One sentence each on: monitoring and forecasting using
computers; recording changes of temperature on volcanoes
(shows magma is rising); recording water levels in wells (shows
ground is moving/tilting in earthquake areas); observing strange
animal behaviour.
b) Six sentences on planning: eg monitoring, predicting and warning
people; informing people of what to do eg store food, batteries,
water; have good planning eg action plans for fire, ambulance,
hospitals; teach drills eg how to behave during an earthquake;
good building design ; have stores of tents, bottled water, food,
ready for emergencies.

Q3 Sample answers : 1. Experts assess how serious the disaster
is. 2. Local people told what to do eg by TV, Radio, or loud
hailers. 3. Injured rescued and taken to hospital, and fires put out.
4. Services must be restored to prevent disease. 5. Lines of
communication must be restored because outside help must get in.

Q4 Ten sentences – eg 1. People don't know what to do – little
planning. 2. Difficult to tell people what to do – communications
are poorer than in MEDCs. 3. LEDCs are often poor – little
money to spend on being prepared for hazards. 4. Dense
populations eg in shanty towns – many killed when buildings
collapse. 5. Difficult to get help – poor communications.
6. Delays lead to more fires, disease, deaths. 7. Foreign aid takes
days/weeks to arrive. 8. Poor medical facilities – more people die
than should. 9. Homelessness and contaminated water cause
more deaths from diseases. 10. Collapse of poorly built houses and
flats kills people.

Pages 7, 8 and 9

Q1 a) Igneous, Sedimentary, Metamorphic.
b) Molten material (magma).
c) Intrusive rocks form when magma is squeezed into the existing
rocks, cooling before reaching the surface. Eg granite.
d) Extrusive rocks form when magma reaches the surface and
becomes lava. Eg basalt.
e) The 4 features are sill (I), dyke (I), volcano (E), batholith (I).

Q2 Correct words are: beds; deposited; sandstone; shale; strata;
bedding plane; calcium carbonate; shells; plants.

Q3 Metamorphic rocks form when sedimentary and igneous rocks are
heated or subjected to pressure. These changes can occur during
volcanic or earthquake activity.

Q4 Harder, more compact, more crystalline.

Q5 Sandstone – Quartzite; Limestone – Marble; Granite – Gneiss;
Clay – Slate.

Q6 a – Metamorphic rocks; b – Granite; c – Clay; d – Sandstone.

Q7 a) eg The Pennines b) eg The North Downs c) Pervious means
rainwater passes into the rock by passing down into joints and
cracks d) Porous means rain water soaks into the air spaces
within the rock, as into a sponge. e) Rivers and streams.

Q8 Cuesta.

Q9 The scarp slope; the dip slope; spring; chalk or limestone.

Pages 10, 11

Q1 Weathering is the breakdown or decomposition of rocks by
physical, chemical and biological processes. It does not include
any movement.

Q2 0°C; winter; water; expands; contracts; weakening; rough/
jagged; scree; gentler; blockfields.

Q3 3 diagrams – one of heating and expansion by day. One of cooling
and contraction of rock by night; third diagram to show that
repeated day/night expansion and contraction leads to shells or
layers of rock falling off like layers of an onion. For example:

Q4 Rotting of rocks by acids in decaying plant remains. Plant roots
prise open cracks in rocks until they break up.

Q5 Correct order is: c) b) d) a)

Q6 i) Pavement – a rocky surface of limestone where the bare rock is
exposed. ii) Clint – a slab of limestone seen on the pavement,
rather like a paving slab. iii) Gryke – a deep groove between the
clints, formed as rain dissolves out a joint

Q7
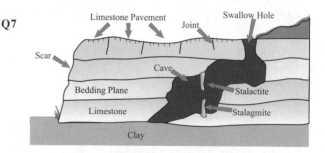

Labels could also include these: scarp slope, dip slope, clints,
grykes, spring.

Q8 China clay (kaolin) — eg in Cornwall.

Page 12

Q1 evaporates; water vapour; rises; cools; condensation; clouds;
rain; snow; hail.

Q2 1. Evaporation and transpiration 2. Percolation 3. Infiltration
4. Interception 5. Surface run off 6. Surface storage
7. Throughflow 8. Groundwater flow.

Q3 The river is large at Worcester – several tributaries have joined the Severn. Their catchment area is very large – so rain falling over a large area has percolated and infiltrated into the ground and flowed by throughflow and groundwater flow into the river. This takes 2 or 3 days to reach Worcester, as does the surface runoff. This is why flooding is likely days after it has stopped raining.

Page 13 - 15

Q1 The area drained by a river and all its tributaries.

Q2 Catchment area.

Q3 The watershed is the high ground that separates two basins. Rainfall falling on the water can run off in opposite directions.

Q4 The Amazon Basin.
a) Missouri and Mississippi confluence **b)** tributary **c)** mouth
d) discharge; sediment.

Q5 **a)** sentence about interception, evaporation and transpiration
b) rainfall is stored in the reservoir
c) rainfall runs off tarmac roads, concrete, and is quickly taken away by drains
d) in summer crops intercept and use the rainfall, in winter if soil is bare, rainfall runs off the surface
e) rain runs off impermeable rock – it cannot soak in.
2 other reasons could be – GRADIENT– steep areas have more rapid runoff so rain reaches F quickly. USE OF WATER – if town uses lots of water for industry, homes, then less water will reach F.

Q6 a) Write about 3 ideas eg. fertile soils and lowland, for farming; supply of fresh water for homes, industry, and farms; water creates HEP; river can be used for transport and for recreation, like fishing and boating; they are attractive areas for people to see, with their wildlife and plants.
b) Write about 3 ideas eg. pollution of the river by industry or sewage; increasing areas of towns cause more run off and flooding; if too much water is used, water levels get too low and fish die; environment destroyed/damaged by building and industry.

Q7 **i)** More rain in the mountains (1500 – 2000 mm/yr); colder in the mountains — less evaporation; upper course valleys are deep and V shaped — easier to construct a dam here.
ii) Valleys too wide and shallow — difficult to build a dam; rocks softer and less stable — can't support weight of reservoir and dam.
iii) 1. To store water for supplies to towns 2. To hold back excess water and reduce flooding 3. To provide water for irrigation and industry.
iv) Woodlands are useful because: 1. They intercept the rain and slow down runoff to river; 2. They hold the soil in place and stop it being washed down into the river, causing more flooding; 3. They are attractive and are homes for wildlife.

Pages 16, 17

Q1 **a)** source **b)** interlocking spurs **c)** waterfall **d)** rapids

Q2 **a)** vertical erosion **b)** winds around hills and harder rock **c)** hard rock **d)** plunge pool.

Q3 *Formation*: hard rock layer, softer one downstream is eroded faster – plunge pool. *Retreat*: overhanging harder rock collapses, causing retreat of falls upstream. A gorge is left.

Q4 eg Niagara Falls, USA. High Force, on River Tees.

Q5 About 5 lines on formation of rapids – hard rock layers are less eroded, and left sticking up so that water is turbulent with lots of overturning and bubbles; there can be several alternate beds of hard and soft rock.

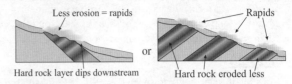

Page 18

Q1 meanders; faster; more; lateral; deeper; river cliff; slower; deposition; point bars; floodplain.

Q2

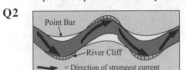

Q3 a – river cliff, erosion b – deeper, faster water c – shallower, slower water d – slip off slope or point bar.

Q4 eg Mississippi; Thames.

Page 19

Q1 **a)** gentle **b)** sediment **c)** floodplain **d)** farming **e)** flat; fertile
f) levees **g)** estuaries **h)** distributaries **i)** deltas

Q2

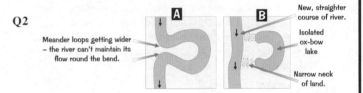

Page 20

Q1 **a)** deposition of fertile alluvium; irrigation water.
b) damage to houses; damage to crops.

Q2 **a)** There was much higher rainfall than normal; the ground was already saturated because of high rainfall in previous weeks; slopes on Exmoor are steep, leading to a rapid runoff; this caused the West and East Lyn Rivers to fill up rapidly and overflow.
b) 34 people died; estimated cost of the damage was £9 million; as the rivers swept material downstream, temporary dams were created, which later burst causing great damage; 1000 people were made homeless, 90 buildings, 150 cars and boats lost.

Q3 Eg. poor planning for emergencies; little spare money for flood defences or aid; people don't know what to do; floodwaters get polluted by animal and human waste, leading to disease; crops and farmland destroyed, leading to starvation.

Pages 21 - 23

Q1 predict; geology and soils; precipitation; short; rapid; likely.

Q2 1. Steep hills can be planted with trees. 2. Crop field can be sown with grass to give cover all winter, and can be ploughed along not up and down, the slope. 3. Towns should leave more open spaces of grass, parks and trees to reduce runoff.

Q3 **i)** Rainfall is higher here – also snow; rocks are hard and can support a dam; valleys are narrow – easier to build dams and reservoirs here; steep slopes cause rapid runoff here, so dams and reservoirs are needed to hold floodwaters.
ii) the river is now much larger, so extra water needs to be held in reservoirs; towns need protection from floods; farmlands need protection from floods.
iii) Beautiful countryside is spoiled; farmland also destroyed when upper valley is flooded.

Q4 Advantages: controls floods; irrigation for crops; river can be used by boats all year; HEP; river levels kept constant all year.
Disadvantages: costly scheme; bilharzia snails increased – disease; less sediment is brought down – it is trapped in the

reservoir – so farmers now have to buy fertiliser; sediment gradually fills up the reservoir; loss of land as reservoir is created.

Q5 dredging; quickly; sea; relief channels; storage areas.

Pages 24 - 25

Q1 a – so a lot of water flows down the Blue Nile in Summer (June to Oct) making floods more likely then.

b – when it rains, runoff is not intercepted and flows rapidly into the river, making it overflow.

c – runoff flows quickly to the rivers, making floods likely.

d – so a lot of water flows down the White Nile (high discharge) all year.

Q2 increase; more; deforestation; decreases; increases; impermeable; infiltrate; steep.

Q3 A flood hydrograph

Q4 1. Peak rainfall 2.Rising limb 3. Peak discharge 4. Falling limb 5. Base flow

Q5 **a)** the time needed for rain to drip from vegetation, to pass into the ground, and then gradually flow to the river as throughflow and groundwater flow.

b) the average or usual flow (discharge) of the river.

Q6 Yes.

Q7 Steep – 5 ideas eg. from heavy rain; impermeable rock; steep slopes; little vegetation; ground already saturated; urban area. Gentle – 5 ideas from: drizzle or gentle rain; permeable rock; gentle slopes; dense woods; dry ground, rural area; after the building of a dam.

Pages 26 - 27

Q1 10 uses could be – drinking; bathing; toilets; washing machines; industry; watering gardens; irrigating crops; swimming pools; washing cars; in the power industry.

Q2 **a)** NW Highlands, Southern Uplands, Lake District, Snowdonia.

b) low population density; little industry.

c) reservoirs; pipelines.

d) hosepipe bans; water meters; educating people; shower rather than bath.

Q3 Summer – farmers need more irrigation for crops; people have more baths and showers when it is hot; people drink more.

Q4 Supply clean water; control and monitor pollution; flood management; look after recreation eg boating and fishing; build dams and reservoirs.

Q5 LEDCs – shortage of clean water (eg India); large and rapidly growing population means demand is growing; many people live without sewage disposal; little money to pay for schemes to provide water or reduce disease from polluted water (Bangladesh).

Q6 self-help; concrete; reduce; evaporation; unpolluted; irrigation; drip feeding.

Pages 28 - 31

Q1 **i)** the wind **ii)** crest **iii)** trough **iv)** wave height **v)** distance between 2 crests, or 2 troughs **vi)** they start to slow down and the top falls forward as the wave breaks **vii)** swash **viii)** backwash **ix)** the distance across open water over which the wave has been travelling **x)** the longer the fetch, the bigger the wave

Q2 Constructive – lower wind speed; approx 1 m high; strong swash; they build up the beach by transporting and depositing material. Destructive – stronger wind; approx. 5 – 6 m high; strong backwash; beach eroded.

Q3 **Corrasion** – waves throw rock particles against the cliffs, scraping them and causing more rock to break off.

Hydraulic Action – waves advance and compress the air and water in rocks in the coastline; then the waves retreat and the air and water can expand with great force, enlarging the cracks and

weakening and breaking off the rocks.

Attrition – the particles are themselves eroded by bumping together in the water, so that they become smaller and more rounded. Rocks become pebbles, which become shingle then sand.

Corrosion – is the solution of rocks by the salty sea water – it involves chemical actions and the rocks rot (eg limestone).

Q4 Longshore drift.

Q5 When the prevailing wind...

Each swash pushes…

Each backwash…

Therefore particles move along...

Q6
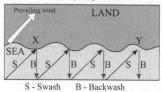

Particle X bounced along coast to Y, by Longshore drift

S - Swash   B - Backwash

Q7 1 – blowhole; 2 – cave; 3 – arch; 4 – stack.

Q8 High tide; notch; unstable; steep; retreating; wave cut platform.

Q9 Rock type.

Q10 True; false.

Headland – eg Hengistbury Head near Bournemouth;

Bay – eg Lulworth Cove, Dorset.

Q11 **Caves** – form where there are cracks and joints. The sea eroded these eg by hydraulic action and abrasion, enlarging the cracks into caves.

Blowholes – form where the cave is eroded upwards along a crack or joint until the roof of the cave comes out on the top of the headland.

Arches – occur where two caves form back to back on a headland, until they are eroded through; or when one cave is eroded through to the other side – this results in an arch in the headland.

Stack – forms when the arch is further eroded and collapses, leaving rocks in the water known as stacks.

Q12 Summary: **i)** Corrasion, Hydraulic Action, Attrition, Corrosion. **ii) Headland** (Hengistbury Head); **cliff** (White Cliffs of Dover; **wave cut platform** (on the beach at Robin Hood's Bay, Yorks); **caves**, **blowholes**, (along the coast at Lulworth Cove, Dorset); **arch** (Durdle Door, Dorset); **stacks** (the Needles, Isle of Wight).

Pages 32 - 33

Q1 **i)** Because these areas are sheltered and the waves slow down as they enter.

ii) Sand; pebbles.

iii) A ridge of shingle and pebbles at the top of a beach. It is deposited here by storm waves usually in winter.

iv) eg Blackpool beach.

Q2 **i)** South West **ii)** East **iii)** the coast turns at an angle at the estuary **iv)** hooks or recurves **v)** muds are deposited here because the waves don't disturb this area, forming mudflats and a salt marsh.

v) eg Orford Ness, Suffolk.

Q3 A tombolo is where a ridge of deposited material joins an island onto the mainland. Eg Chesil Beach, in Dorset.

Q4

Pages 33 – 43

This lagoon slowly silts up to become a marsh. An example of this is Slapton Sands, Devon.

Q5 **Beach** – eg Blackpool; **Spit** – eg Orford Ness; **Tombolo** – eg Chesil Beach; **Barrier Beach** – eg Slapton Sands.

Pages 34 - 35

Q1 A - sea wall; B – groynes; C – armour blocks; D – gabions.

Q2 Revetments

Q3 **Sea wall**: Advantages – reduce erosion and flooding; people feel safer. Disadvantages – costly (can be £2000 per metre); are eventually undermined and broken by wave erosion; wave energy deflected and this can cause more erosion of beach material; ugly. **Groynes**: Advantages – reduce longshore drift and so keep the beach in place. The protection of the beach also reduces erosion of cliffs. Disadvantages – costly (£6000 each; made of wood which rots in sea water. **Armour blocks**: Advantages – cheap; reduce erosion and protect foot of cliffs. Disadvantages – ugly, tourists don't like them on the beach. **Gabions**: Advantages – cheap, reduce erosion. Disadvantages – ugly and unnatural looking.

Q4 They can trample areas, destroying vegetation and features. (or could write about litter; or about the need for car parks, access roads etc.)

Q5 **Manage coastal areas** by eg National Trust; **have organised car parks, access paths, leaflets** to reduce damage; **fence off areas** of fragile vegetation.

Q6 Conflicts: **Farmers** are losing land as cliffs erode, and want sea defences, but **conservationists** want coastal areas to be left as natural areas eg for birds. **Tourists** want nice beaches – they don't like the look of many of the sea defences. **Fishermen** are concerned about sea pollution, which may come from pleasure boats. **Residents** want their coastline to be protected, but **conservationists** argue that sea walls, armour etc may cover up nest sites, important plants.

Pages 36 - 38

Q1 a) Ice Ages b) 10,000 yrs ago c) glaciers d) plucking. Abrasion is the scouring of the land by a scraping action using the rocks embedded in the ice. Plucking is when the ice freezes around rocks by entering the cracks, and then moves on, tearing the rocks out e) freeze thaw f) on top of the ice, under it, and within it g) deposition h) lowlands i) snout.

Q2 a) mountain/upland b) down c) high, low.
d) slowly e) V, U.

Q3 A - corrie (or cirque / cwm), B – glacier, C – arete,
D – pyramidal peak.

Q4 rotational slip; abrasion; plucking; corrie; B; tarn; steep; arete; freeze thaw; pyramidal.

Q5 A: eg Red Tarn, Helvellyn; C: eg Striding Edge, Helvellyn;
D: eg The Matterhorn.

Q6 i) U ii) truncated spurs iii) hanging valleys ,waterfalls
iv) eg the Nant Ffrancon valley in Wales.

Q7 Glaciers eroded softer rocks out of the valley floor, by abrasion and plucking. These areas became deepened as rock basins, which were long and narrow, following the shape of the valley. They filled with water, and are now called Ribbon Lakes.
E.g. Lake Windermere in the Lake District.

Q8 Glacier eroded and scoured one side of upstanding harder rocks in their path, and plucked the downstream side, leaving this jagged.

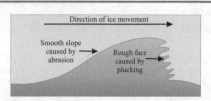

Q9 Arete; Corrie; Tarn; Pyramidal Peak; Hanging Valley; Waterfall; Truncated Spur; Ribbon Lake; Glaciated Valley; Roche Moutonnee.

Page 39

Q1 When the glacier melts.

Q2 b)

Q3 A – Terminal Moraine; B – Medial Moraine; C – Lateral Moraine;
D – Drumlins; E – Erratics; F – Ground Moraine.

Q4 A – Deposition of boulder clay at the snout, where material carried was dumped due to the ice melting; E – Rocks that have been transported far from their original location; D – Mounds of boulder clay were deposited under the ice, then the moving ice shaped them into rounded hills, with the pointed end pointing downstream.

Q5 Outwash; organised; sand; eskers; kames; ice; kettle.

Pages 40 - 41

Q1 Slopes too steep for crops – so sheep are kept; too cold, wet, cloudy for crops; glacial erosion has removed soil, so vegetation is poor – only suitable for sheep grazing, e.g. Highlands of Scotland.

Q2 Diversify means to do other things to increase their income eg. take Bed and Breakfast guests, or have caravan sites.

Q3 Because they are flat, and there are deposits of fertile boulder clay (till).

Q4 National Parks. eg Snowdonia, Lake District.

Q5 Beautiful scenery – mountains, valleys, waterfalls, lakes.
Good areas for walking, climbing, sailing and other activities.

Q6 Deep; U; hard; heavy; drier; South.

Q7 i) ….farmland will be flooded.
ii) …gates are left open, paths eroded, walls broken by people climbing over.
iii)…this causes litter, noise, damage to vegetation, disturbance to wildlife.
iv) ...another could be recreation (boating, fishing) versus the Water Authorities, who want to keep the water unpolluted.

Pages 42 - 43

Q1 Temperature (max and min) and precipitation (total, and seasonal distribution).

Q2 a) 16 ℃; b) 5 ℃; c) 11 ℃; d) no; e) winter.

Q3 Temperatures usually fall, because the sun's angle is lower and in winter there is little daylight. Also the yearly temperature range increases.

Q4 Temperatures usually fall with height; rainfall increases (relief rain).

Q5 a) In summer inland areas are warmer than coasts; b) inland areas are colder than coasts in winter. c) This is because land areas heat up and cool down quickly, whereas sea areas heat up and cool down slowly.

Q6 Inland.

Q7 Rain decreases, because as distance from the sea increases, winds will have lost their moisture.

Q8 Continentality.

Q9 Winds from a warm area bring higher temperatures, and from a dry area bring dry weather. Winds from colder areas bring lower temperatures, and winds from the sea (onshore winds) bring wetter weather.

Pages 43 – 52

Q10 The Westerly wind belt.

Q11 **a)** Latitude; **b)** Altitude; **c)** Continentality; **d)** Prevailing Winds; **e)** Position.

Q12 hot; small; 2; high; all year round; Equatorial.

Q13 Tundra.

Q14 Winter.

Pages 44 - 45

Q1 Precipitation is the correct word for moisture that falls from clouds – eg rain, snow; sleet; hail.

Q2 saturated; dew point; condense; clouds; precipitation; Convectional; Frontal.

Q3

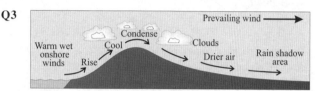

Q4 **a)** The Rain Shadow is the area on the other side of the hills where the air is descending and warming, so that these areas are drier due to evaporation of any clouds and because most of the moisture has fallen over the hills.
b) Lake District -Relief Rain; **c) Yorkshire** – Rain Shadow.

Q5 Convectional Rain.
Warm; rises; convection; rises; cools; condenses; thick; cumulonimbus; heavy rain; thunder and lightning.

Q6 **a)** a boundary between cold and warm air.
b) heavy showery rain.
c) drizzle and steady rain.
d) lows (depressions).
e) eg Britain.

Pages 46 - 47

Q1 **a)** Temperature; air pressure; rainfall; wind. **b)** Weather map.
c) The weight of air per unit area of the surface of the earth.
d) isobars. **e)** millibars.

Q2 ● rain   ※ snow showers   ═ mist

      ❥ drizzle   ⏃ thunderstorm

Q3 Southwesterly wind; temperature of 6°C; rain showers; sky 6/8 covered with cloud; wind speed 18 – 22 knots (moderate breeze).

Q4 **A** – a low or depression; **B** – a high or anticyclone.

Q5 They give a good overall view of the world's current weather; they can show temperatures in various places; they show clouds etc.

Q6 White.

Q7 Black.

Pages 48 - 49

Q1 West; tropical maritime; south; polar; north; polar front; less dense; low; fronts; north east.

Q2

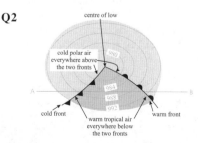

Q3 cold; cirrus; drizzle and rain; warm; rise; stops; cold; ahead of; heavy; cold; polar; veer.

Q4 Cold air at the back of the depression travels faster than the warm air in front of it. So it catches it up, and being denser, undercuts it and lifts it off the ground, causing clouds and rain. This is called an occlusion.

Q5 **a)** false; **b)** false; **c)** true; **d)** false; **e)** true; **f)** true.

Q6 Skies are clear, so heat escapes from earth at night, and this chills the air next to the ground, causing it to become saturated with moisture. When it becomes very cold (below 0°C) this moisture freezes, as frost.

Q7 When the temperature near the ground is colder than it is higher up, this is called a temperature inversion. Fogs form in this cold air, and this is often known as "anticyclonic gloom".

Q8

Feature	Depressions	Anticyclone
Air Pressure	Low in middle	High in middle
Winds	Higher	Lower
Cloudiness	Greater	Less
Temps (summer)	Lower	Higher
Temps (winter)	Higher	Lower
Rain	Lots	Little

Page 50

Q1 Low.

Q2 Tropical cyclone – India; (or willy willies – Australia; or typhoons – Pacific).

Q3 b)

Q4 Summer and autumn.

Q5 warm; 26°C; evaporates; rise; vortex; condenses; huge; very strong; 160; poles; colder; land.

Q6 **a)** eye; **b)** 30 – 50 km; **c)** dry, calm and warm; **d)** falling.

Q7 80.

Q8 20 000.

Q9 Japan; Australia; Caribbean; China; Bangladesh.

Pages 51 - 52

Q1 droplets of water; lower; condensation; water vapour; smoke.

Q2 Advection fog forms when warm moist air moves over a cold surface eg a cold sea. The warm air is cooled, condensation occurs in the air forming fog. Eg at San Francisco, California in summer.

Q3 **a)** Rain and drizzle falls from the warm tropical air which is rising above the cold air at a warm front. This rain and drizzle causes the cold air below to become saturated, so that condensation occurs as fog.
b) Frontal fog.

Q4 **a)** clear. **b)** radiation. **c)** dew point. **d)** condense. **e)** wind.
f) Radiation Fog. **g)** Autumn, winter. Not usually summer.

Q5 Steam fog forms where cold air lies above warmer water. Rising air with water vapour meets the cold air, is cooled, causing condensation as a fog which look like steam rising over the water. Eg over Arctic seas.

Q6 **a)** smog is dirty and has smoke and pollution particles in it.
b) urban. **c)** dust, smoke, and pollution particles; they help and speed up condensation. **d)** eg Los Angeles.

Q7 Dangerous driving conditions; breathing difficulties. (Could also say dangers to shipping, or air travel.)

Pages 53 – 65

Pages 53 - 55

Q1 The local differences in climate within small areas.

Q2 **a)** Temperatures in centre are 14°C, which is 4 degrees warmer than the rural areas on the edge of the city.
b) "The urban heat island effect".
c) Buildings absorb Sun's heat by day, and release it at night; central heating; heat trapped in the city at night, because of the pollution which lies over it. (Also factories; lights).
d) Night – because earth is cooling down in other areas where there is less pollution, so warmth in city is more noticeable; more central heating and lights.
e) U.S cities have denser buildings, taller buildings.

Q3 Because not all Sun's rays can't all get through the pollution.

Q4 More – because pollution and dust act as condensation nuclei.

Q5 Buildings slow down average wind speeds; however along streets of tall buildings, there is a wind tunnel effect with strong gusty winds.

Q6 **a)** B – due to shelter of trees; **b)** A – because there is no shade; **c)** B – because heat is trapped by the forest; **d)** A – because there is no/little vegetation to provide moisture by transpiration; because sun and wind dry out area A and there is no shelter/shade. **e)** B – because of the dark colour.

Q7

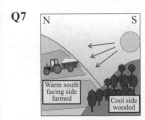

Q8 **a)** More water is evaporating into the air; air is cooler leading to condensation; **b)** They are smoother surfaces, less friction; **c)** Cooler; **d)** Warmer; **e)** Because water areas heat up slowly compared to land, and cool down slowly too.

Q9 Urban and Rural; Colour; Aspect; Water; Land; Vegetation.

Q10 **a)** (maximum and minimum) thermometer **b)** rain gauge **c)** wind vane.

Q11 **a)** air pressure **b)** wind speed.

Page 56

Q1 ….living things, …..environment.

Q2 biomes.

Q3 **a)** Tropical Rain Forest; **b)** Temperate Deciduous Forest; **c)** Tundra.

Q4 Climate; Relief; Geology; Soils.

Page 57

Q1 eg Sahara; Gobi.

Q2 Very low rainfall totals; rain varies at lot each year and so it is unreliable.

Q3 3 of: Small spiky leaves to reduce water loss by transpiration; long roots often down to the water table; stems and trunk can swell with stored water like cacti; thick waxy stems to reduce water loss; some plants survive as seeds, and when it rains these are adapted to grow, flower and seed again in only a few days.

Q4 near the poles; North Canada; low; low; windy; frozen; permafrost; short; small; below 30 cm.

Q5 mosses and lichens which grow near to the ground; taller grasses; stunted bushes and trees eg Arctic willow and birch; short lived flowering plants which form bright carpets called "bloom mats" eg poppies.

Pages 58 - 59

Q1 **a)** Equatorial **b)** eg Amazonia **c)** Temperatures are very high all year (around 27°C) and rainfall is high all year (can be 2500 mm/yr) **d)** no definite seasons **e)** some plants can be flowering, others can be having fruit, at the same time in the same area **f)** trees **g)** starfish **h)** large, thick, waxy, with drip tips to let rain run off (otherwise transpiration will stop and photosynthesis becomes difficult) **i)** many different ones.

Q2 **a)** Layer A: canopy; Layer B: lower tree layer; Layer C: undergrowth **b)** emergents; 50 m **c)** umbrella shaped, so that they are spreading out to catch as much light as possible **d)** buttress roots – to support the trees which are very tall **e)** very low **f)** little grows on the rain forest floor, because it is too dark making photosynthesis difficult **g)** orchids and climbers (lianas).

Page 60

Q1 North and South; Kenya and Ethiopia; definite wet and dry seasons; grasses; tough and spiky; tall; 3m; pampas; a lot of; die down.

Q2 Stems and trunk can swell, storing water; roots are long to search for water deep underground; leaves are small and spiky to reduce water loss, eg. baobab tree.

Q3 Humans have affected the vegetation e.g. by burning it and grazing animals, so that the vegetation is changed from its original state.

Page 61

Q1 **a)** false; **b)** true; **c)** true; **d)** false **e)** false **f)** true.

Q2 Italy and Greece; 30 – 40°N and S; hot and dry; grazing; evergreen forest; drought; thorny shrubs; thyme; very small; reduce.

Page 62

Q1 eg Britain, Western Europe, E. USA.

Q2 Plants shed their leaves in the winter cold.

Q3 **a)** The tree layer has deciduous trees such as oak and ash. **b)** The shrub layer is made of deciduous bushes such as hazel and hawthorn. **c)** The ground cover is made of spring flowers such as bluebells, and grasses.

Page 63

Q1 Harsh.

Q2 Northern N. America, and Northern Asia.

Q3

Feature	Description	Reason
Tree	Evergreen	Can grow immediately in spring, without having to grow buds.
Shape	Conical	Lets snow slide off
Branches	Flexible	To let snow slide off without damaging tree
Roots	Shallow	Ground is frozen in winter
Leaves	Needles	To reduce water loss
Cones		To protect the seeds

Q4 Pine, fir. (Or any other suitable answer.)

Q5 Because little light reaches the forest floor, and because the needles make the soil very acidic.

Page 64

Q1 **a)** minerals **b)** 45% **c)** 25% **d)** 25% **e)** organic matter e.g. leaves, decomposed matter called humus, bacteria, worms.

Q2 Red and yellow.

Q3 Clay.

Page 65

Q1 **Leaching**: rainfall; soluble; less.
Podsolisation: coniferous; more; paler; pale ash-grey; darker;

Pages 65 – 77

red-brown; infertile.

Q2 **a)** True; **b)** True.

Q3 The lack of oxygen in gley soils causes ferric iron oxide (which is red/brown) to change to ferrous iron (which is blue/grey).

Q4 **a)** high temperatures cause strong evaporation which draws up the water to the surface; **b)** salts are precipitated from this water.

Page 66

Q1 **a)** 14 **b)** acidic **c)** alkaline.

Q2 Ferric iron.

Q3 Texture describes the particle sizes in the soil, e.g. sandy.

Q4 Structure.

Q5 **a)** near the surface – dead leaves and humus; next layer down – upper soil, fertile, brown colour, crumb structure. Lowest layer – parent rock. **b)** Brown earth **c)** Temperate deciduous forest; eg Britain.

Page 67

Q1 Rabbit / mouse.

Q2 Primary producers; the Sun; photosynthesis; soil; sheep; carnivores.

Q3 Carbon Dioxide + Water + Sunlight = Sugar + Water + Oxygen.

Q4 **a)** industrial areas burn coal, oil, gas, which all contain carbon, in factories and power stations. **b)** if trees are felled, they no longer use carbon dioxide in photosynthesis. Also if trees are burned, they contain carbon, which is released into the air.

Q5

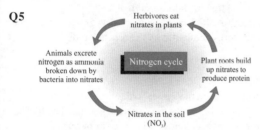

Herbivores eat
nitrates in plants

Animals excrete
nitrogen as ammonia
broken down by
bacteria into nitrates

Nitrogen cycle

Plant roots build
up nitrates to
produce protein

Nitrates in the soil
(NO_3)

Q6 They decompose them and this releases nutrients into the soil, so that they can be re-used.

Page 68

Q1 **a)** for farming; for building towns and cities **b)** for cereal farming; burning by Indians to remove trees on land that they used for grazing.

Q2 Vegetation that has reached its full development, and is in equilibrium with its environment.

Q3 One that is disturbed by humans eg. by grazing their animals, so that the vegetation changes and no longer develops as it should.

Q4 Tundra.

Q5 **a)** deforestation; growing population **b)** steep; Himalayas **c)** run off; soil erosion **d)** Ganges **e)** flooding; Bangladesh.

Page 69

Q1 Tropical Rain Forest.

Q2 Large scale destruction by logging of hardwoods eg. mahogany – timber sold to MEDCs for furniture; trees not replaced. Huge areas destroyed.

Rapid growth of population in Brazil – government has encouraged poor people to settle in Amazonia, and has built roads into the forest. This has led to deforestation of large areas.

Many areas have been cleared for cattle ranches by big companies, who want to get rich. But farming, and grazing don't succeed because the soil loses its fertility.

Deforestation for mining – eg. at Carajas in Brazil is the world's largest reserve of iron ore. Iron ore is exported to MEDCs to help

pay off Brazil's foreign debt.

Huge areas have been destroyed by flooding of land for HEP developments.

Logging companies that don't plant trees to replace those they take also results in large areas being lost.

Q3 **a)** Oil and gas **b)** Pollution from oil spills **c)** No – because it is very difficult for plants to start again and grow in such a cold, harsh area.

Pages 70

Q1 Soils only stay fertile while the trees are there (they shed leaves and fruit which decay and add nutrients to the soil, and the trees shelter the soil from the heavy rain).

Q2 Medicines can sometimes be made from chemicals found in the plants.

Q3 Because it is their home and their source of food.

Q4 **a)** Trees use carbon dioxide in photosynthesis, helping to prevent the increase in CO_2 levels that cause global warming **b)** It leads to less evapotranspiration, which means less rainfall.

Pages 71

Q1 **1)** L; M. **2)** L; M. **3)** M; L.

Q2 MEDCs could stop buying rainforest products; MEDCs could cancel debts owed to them by LEDCs.

Q3 Malaysia's government strictly controls the timber industry. One third of the world's hardwood exports come from here, but trees have to be a certain height and age before they are felled, and all felled trees have to be replaced by newly planted ones.

Pages 76, 77

Q1 **a)** 3189 **b)** Hurst Castle **c)** cliffs

d)

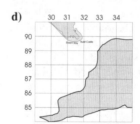

Q2 **a)** map 1: upper stage, map 2: lower stage, map 3: lower stage, map 4: upper stage, map 5: lower stage, map 6: upper stage.

b) accept 108661 or 109661

c) ox-bow lake

d) Left to right

Q3 **a)** meander **b)** waterfall **c)** height, steep, closer, steeper

d)

Mellbreak

Grasmoor

e) a glacier

f) corrie

g) Ice in hollows causes plucking and freeze thaw which steepens the back and side walls. The ice moves with a circular motion known as rotational slip which deepens the hollow into a bowl.